AF815268

Developing Asian BONDMARKETS

Developing Asian BONDMARKETS

Takatoshi Ito &
Yung Chul Park
(eds)

Australian National University

E PRESS

Published by ANU E Press
The Australian National University
Canberra ACT 0200, Australia
Email: anuepress@anu.edu.au
This title is also available online at http://epress.anu.edu.au

National Library of Australia Cataloguing-in-Publication entry

Title: Developing Asian bondmarkets / edited by Takatoshi Ito and Yung Chul Park.

ISBN: 9781925021394 (paperback) 9781925021400 (ebook)

Subjects: Bond market--Asia.
Bond market--East Asia.
Monetary policy--Asia.
Monetary policy--East Asia.
Bonds.

Other Authors/Contributors:
Ito, Takatoshi, 1950-, editor.
Park, Yung Chul, editor.

Dewey Number: 332.6323

Printed by Griffin Press

Contents

Tables

Appendix tables

Figures

Appendix figures

Abbreviations in tables

n.a. not applicable
. not available
- zero
. insignificant

Abbreviations

ABC	Asian basket currency
ABF	Asian Bond Fund
ABS	asset-backed security
ADB	Asian Development Bank
ADM	Asian Dollar Market
CBO	collateralised bond obligation
CDO	collateralised debt obligation
CLO	collateralised loan obligation
CMI	Chiang Mai Initiative
CMO	collateralised mortgage obligation
CMU	Central Moneymarkets Units
CPF	Central Provident Fund
CRA	credit-rating agency
ECU	European currency unit
EMEAP	Executives' Meeting of East Asia and Pacific Central Banks
HKMA	Hong Kong Monetary Authority
IAG	International Advisory Group
IAS	international accounting standards
IMF	International Monetary Fund
JBIC	Japan Bank for International Cooperation
MAS	Monetary Authority of Singapore
MBB	Municipal bond bank
MTN	medium-term note
PECC	Pacific Economic Cooperation Council
RTGS	real time gross settlement

Contributors

Richard Yan-Ki Ho

Richard Yan-Ki Ho obtained his MS and PhD degree from the University of Wisconsin-Madison. He is the Professor of Finance in the Department of Economics and Finance at City University of Hong Kong. He was Dean of the Faculty of Business at City University of Hong Kong from 1995 to 2001. Before joining the City University, Professor Ho also worked at the Chinese University of Hong Kong and the Hong Kong Baptist University. He was appointed as member of the Insider Dealing Tribunal of the Government of Hong Kong (1994–95), a part-time member of the Central Policy Unit, Government of HKSAR (1998–2000), and a member of the Economic Advisory Committee of the Financial Secretary's Office (2000–01). He is a member of the Executive Committee of the Hong Kong Institute of Bankers and a member of the Small and Medium Enterprises Committee of the Government of HKSAR.

Takatoshi Ito

Takatoshi Ito is a professor at the Graduate School of Economics at the University of Tokyo. He has taught at Hitotsubashi University, University of Minnesota and Harvard University. He also held the position of Senior Advisor in the Research Department, International Monetary Fund from 1994 to 1997 and Deputy Vice Minister for International Affairs at the Ministry of Finance, Japan from 1999 to 2001). He is an author of many books including *The Japanese Economy* (MIT Press, 1992), *The Political Economy of the Japanese Monetary Policy* and *Financial Policy and Central Banking in Japan* (both with T. Cargill and M. Hutchison).

Daekeun Park

Daekeun Park is a professor of economics at Hanyang University. He received his BA in economics from Seoul National University in 1981 and went on to receive PhD in economics from Harvard University in 1989. He served as an assistant professor at State University of New York at Albany and was appointed as assistant professor at Hanyang University in 1991, where he served as the department chair from 1994 to 1996 and was promoted to professor in 2000. During 2000–01, he was a visiting scholar at the Center for International Development at Harvard University. His major research areas include savings behaviour, the Asian currency crisis, international capital flows and cross-border fixed income securities investment.

Yung Chul Park

Yung Chul Park is a professor of economics at Korea University. He is also a member of the National Economic Advisory Council. He was an ambassador for International Economy and Trade for the Ministry of Foreign Affairs and Trade from 2001 to 2002 and also chairman of the board, the Korea Exchange Bank in Seoul, 1999–2001. He previously served as the chief economic adviser to President Doo Hwan Chun of Korea, as president of the Korea Development Institute, as president of the Korea Institute Finance, and as a member of the Bank of Korea's Monetary Board. He was director of the Institute of Economic Research at Korea University, taught at Harvard University and Boston University as a visiting professor and worked for the International Monetary Fund. After completing undergraduate work at Seoul National University, he received his PhD from the University of Minnesota. From June to December of 1998, he managed the merger of Korea's two largest commercial banks as chairman of the CBK-Hanil Bank Merger Committee.

S. Ghon Rhee

S. Ghon Rhee is the K.J. Luke Distinguished Professor of International Finance and Banking and serves as the Executive Director of the Asia-Pacific Financial Markets Research Center at the University of Hawaii. He is currently serving as the managing editor of the Pacific Basin Finance Journal and as a member of the US National Committee for Pacific Economic Cooperation (USNCPEC). He is a founding member of the Asian Financial Regulatory Shadow Committee. He holds a PhD in Finance from Ohio State University. He has edited or authored 17 books on Asian financial markets and published over 70 academic papers.

Jorge E. Roldos

Jorge E. Roldos is Deputy Division Chief at the Emerging Markets Surveillance Division of the International Monetary Fund's International Capital Markets Department. He was previously a Senior Economist at the Research Department of the International Monetary Fund. He has also worked as Senior Researcher at CERES (Centro de Estudios de la Realidad Económica y Social), in Montevideo, Uruguay, and as an Advisor at the Planning Office of Uruguay. He has also been a consultant to The World Bank, and to the UNDP Economic Commission for Latin America. His major areas of research are on stabilisation policies, banking and capital markets in emerging market economies.

Gregory R. Stone

Gregory R. Stone is currently a PhD (Finance) candidate at the University of Hawaii. He holds Master degrees from the Colorado School of Mines and the Advanced National School of Petroleum and Engines in Paris. He has previously worked in the investment banking industry. Mr Stone's research interests are in corporate finance, bankruptcy, market microstructures and bondmarkets.

Hung Q. Tran

Hung Q. Tran is Deputy Director of the International Capital Markets Department at the International Monetary Fund, with responsibility for the *Global Financial Stability Report*, a semi-annual publication providing a regular assessment of global financial markets and to identify potential systemic weaknesses that could lead to crisis. Prior to joining the International Monetary Fund in October 2001, Mr Tran was Managing Director of Global Research/ Chief Economist for Rabobank International (London) and Deutsche Bank (New York, Frankfurt, and Singapore). He was also a senior research executive for Solomon Brothers and Merrill Lynch in New York.

Michael Chak Sham Wong

Michael Wong is a Director of the MSc(Banking) and MSc(Financial Engineering) programs of City University of Hong Kong. He is a prolific researcher on investment, risk management and international business and is well connected to the finance and banking community. He has served as a consultant on Basel II implementation of SAS Institute, and an examination committee member of the Hong Kong Securities Institute (HKSI), the Hong Kong Institute of Bankers (HKIB) and the Global Association of Risk Professionals (GARP). Also, he has been a non-Executive Director of Bank of Communications Trustee Ltd.

Foreword

This volume is a collection of the papers submitted to the second annual conference of the Finance Forum of the Pacific Economic Cooperation Council. The papers have been edited after the conference so that they collectively complement each other in providing important information on Asian bonds.

The Standing Committee of the Pacific Economic Cooperation Council (PECC) agreed to create the Finance Forum at its meeting held in Hong Kong in November 2001, as part of the effort to realign its various existing task forces. With this decision, cooperation for financial stability and development in the APEC region finally came to receive the full recognition it deserved. I had the honour of being asked by the Standing Committee to serve as the founding Coordinator of the Forum as well as the Chairman of its International Advisory Group. The Finance Forum, together with its International Advisory Group, was organised in early 2002 and launched its first two-year work program under the broad exploratory theme of *Issues and Challenges for Regional Financial Cooperation in the Asia-Pacific*. This work program was naturally focused on the lessons from the financial crisis of 1997–98 for financial cooperation among East Asian economies, and identified as one of the specific issues for exploration in the second year of the program the case for the development of regional bondmarkets in East Asia.

Since the financial crisis, the development of local bondmarkets has been a major objective of financial reforms in many East Asian economies in recognition of the fact that the absence of vibrant bondmarkets was one of the major causes of the crisis. In parallel with these efforts, there also have been repeated calls for developing regional bondmarkets in East Asia and the regional economies have begun to explore and promote a number of specific initiatives for this purpose, including the Asian Bond Fund (ABF) and the Asian Bond Market Initiative, and various forums such as APEC, the Executives' Meeting of East Asia and Pacific Central Banks (EMEAP) and ASEAN+3. Likewise, there is a large and growing literature on regional bondmarkets in East Asia. Ironically, however, there is little consensus on what exactly the Asian bondmarkets are, and to the extent that an agreement on this definitional issue can be said to exist, on whether they are truly needed in East Asia, whether they can be created as viable markets in the competitive environment of the global economy, or how they should be created as well as what should be the role for intergovernmental cooperation in the context of the answer to this question.

Considering the enthusiasm of many regional economies including Thailand, Korea, and Hong Kong, in particular, and advised by several members of the International Advisory Group, there was a pressing need to undertake a systematic examination of these issues with analytic rigor as well as to solicit a new creative input from academic experts into the constructive policy development process, and Professor Yung Chul Park of Korea University in Seoul was requested to prescribe for the Forum a team research project that would answer this need. Professor Park was kind enough to honour this request and the project so conceived was undertaken in early 2003, drawing the participation of several of the best experts on the subject matter in the APEC region as authors of six component papers. These papers were presented and discussed at the Second Annual Conference of the PECC Finance Forum that was held in Hua Hin, Thailand, on 8–9 July 2003. The present volume consists of these papers as edited by Professors Takatoshi Ito of Tokyo University and Yung Chul Park of Korea University, together with their Overview.

As the project coordinator, I am pleased and honoured to have worked to bring this research to the attention of the policy authorities of the ASEAN+3 and other APEC governments which have been either leading or supporting the effort to develop regional bondmarkets in East Asia, as well as experts in the finance industry or in academia who are interested in the subject matter. I am particularly proud to note that this research raises a number of new and provocative issues as well as specific creative proposals and believe that it contributes to the broadening of the thought horizon on how to develop Asian bondmarkets. I hope that readers of this volume, especially those from the policymaking authorities in the region intent on the development of those markets, will find this publication both timely and helpful.

I would like to express my appreciation of their contributions to this volume to all participants in the Second Annual Conference of the Forum, to the authors of the individual papers as well as both editors of the volume, to all Member Committees of PECC that have made this project possible through their support for the work of the Finance Forum, particularly Korea National Committee for Pacific Economic Cooperation (KOPEC) and Japan National Committee for Pacific Economic Cooperation (JANCPEC), which have provided extra financial support for the preparation of the volume. On behalf of the PECC, I also would like to express my special gratitude to Asia Pacific Press for agreeing to publish this volume. Finally, I would like to acknowledge the very valuable contribution of Ms Eunsuk Lee, Assistant Director of KOPEC, without whose assistance I would not have been able to carry the work of the Finance Forum thus far, as well as this publication project, to a successful conclusion.

Soogil Young
Coordinator, Pacific Economic Cooperation Council Finance Forum
April 2004, Seoul

1 Overview

Challenges and strategies

Takatoshi Ito and Yung Chul Park

Asian bonds are the interest-bearing obligations of Asian governments, corporations or financial institutions, wherever they are marketed or in whatever currency they are denominated. Asian bonds are defined by the residence of the issuer. But, many advocates and policymakers presume that Asian bonds will be denominated in Asian currencies. A regional bondmarket in Asia would be primarily defined as bringing together issuers and investors from Asia. The ASEAN+3 Finance Ministers' process has established six working groups to tackle issues considered obstacles in promoting the Asian bondmarket under the banner of the Asian Bond Markets Initiative.

One of the lessons from the Asian currency crisis was that too much borrowing in US dollars increased the vulnerability of a country. When the direction of capital flows reverse, a country may find itself in a dollar-liquidity crisis, even though that country may be solvent. At the time of the crisis, massive capital outflows were possible because capital that had come in earlier was in short-term flows. A 'double mismatch'—currency mismatch and maturity mismatch—characterised the problem of financial institutions and corporations in East Asia. In order to avoid another crisis in the future, Asian financial institutions and corporations have to develop a long-term funding source denominated in local currency to match investment needs. Local-currency denominated bond financing solves the double mismatch problem. There is little doubt that deep and liquid domestic bondmarkets will help reduce the severity of the double mismatch in the future. However Asian bond proponents argue that Asian regional bondmarkets could also mitigate the problem.

Although the importance of bondmarkets in the region has been recognised by policymakers, no concrete action has yet been taken. The issue rose to centre stage in policy discussions when it became a part of regional policy initiatives supported by Prime Minister Thaksin of Thailand in 2002. After his call for Asian bonds, several actions were taken both in the Central Bank Forum and the Ministry of Finance process. One such effort materialised as the Asian Bond Fund, established in June 2003 by eleven central banks in the region (the Executives' Meeting of East Asia and Pacific Central Banks Group). The fund was established by foreign reserves contributions invested in dollar-denominated bonds issued by governments and government agencies in Asia. Since foreign reserves are used for this fund, riskier bonds are not included in the investment portfolio. Some sceptics point out that substitution of dollar-denominated US bonds by dollar-denominated Asian bonds may not have a strong impact to help issue Asian bonds in the local currency. In response, it has been proposed that when the next attempt to create a similar fund's made the central banks should purchase local-currency denominated government bonds.

Other initiatives include several private sector and official sector proposals, encouraging issues of Asian local-currency denominated corporate bonds and asset-backed securities.

Proposals include the following aspects. In order to invite participation of investors from the countries in the region, domestic bondmarkets should be open to foreigners. Credit-rating companies in Asian countries should be encouraged to cover bonds of other countries in the region, either by research or by affiliation. Another idea is to bundle together some of the local-currency denominated bonds, so that currency and credit risks are diversified for investors.

Before the 1997–98 Asian crisis, government bondmarkets were very small and illiquid, largely because Asian countries were prudent in managing their government finances. In Korea, Malaysia, Singapore and Thailand, government bonds were not issued simply because they were not needed. In Malaysia and Singapore, large surpluses were recorded in public pension fund accounts. Including these public pension funds, the governments were running large surpluses. In Indonesia, the regular budget was largely balanced, while another budget for development projects existed, and official lending of multilateral institutions and bilateral sources financed the budget.

When the Asian currency crisis occurred in the summer and autumn of 1997, it quickly became the East Asian financial crisis, as many banks (with double mismatch) became insolvent. Foreign investors refused rollovers of short-term lending in US dollars, so that banks in the emerging market economies, most typically in Korea, had to find US dollars to meet their obligation. Foreign reserves were quickly depleted and the crisis deepened. Even the International Monetary Fund (IMF) program did not calm investors.

This episode was pointed out as *prima facie* evidence of the desirability of bond financing in local currencies. Had borrowing of corporations and banks been denominated in local currencies, the US dollar liquidity crisis could have been averted. It is also often argued that if borrowings of corporations and banks had been in long-term bonds, even if they were denominated in US dollars, the acute dollar liquidity crisis might not have happened. The importance of having the domestic bondmarket was pointed out immediately after the East Asian financial crisis.

The scenery has changed dramatically in the wake of the financial crises of 1997–98. Several governments in the region were forced to issue a large amount of government bonds to finance fiscal deficits and bank recapitalisation. Even after increased bond financing, the bondmarkets in East Asia, both domestic and regional, remain relatively small, inactive and illiquid. An inefficient market is not attractive to global bond investors.

Since the domestic bondmarket was not emphasised as an important channel of government and industrial financing, market infrastructure is not well developed. Legal and regulatory aspects of bondmarkets in Asian countries have remained opaque. Protection of minority investors is questionable, and trading and settlement is costly. This, together with the low standard of accounting, auditing and disclosure, has hampered the supply of high quality corporate bonds. Weak corporate governance has also discouraged investors to hold corporate bonds in their portfolios. Most of all, a myriad of regulations on issuance and transactions of bonds has in effect closed the markets to foreign investors and borrowers, and left little room for bondmarkets to flourish in Asian financial systems.

There are several regional bondmarkets where, in theory, Asian borrowers can issue bonds denominated in their domestic currency as well as in major currencies, such as the Samurai and Shogun markets in Japan. In Hong Kong SAR and Singapore offshore markets, issuance and transactions of bonds can be carried out more efficiently than in many domestic markets.

In Singapore, there is an offshore Asian dollar market where Asian bonds, denominated in US dollars, are issued and traded. However, these markets were not active when compared to vibrant bondmarkets in the United States or in Europe. Potential needs for bond financing of Asian governments and corporations did not materialise in these markets, even after the East Asian financial crises.

If no action is taken, the current scope for Asian bondmarket development is limited. However, many consider that with careful preparation market infrastructure at national and regional levels, the issuance and trading of bonds by Asian governments and corporations will increase.

Overview

Park and Park (Chapter 2) propose a market-oriented approach to the development of Asian bondmarkets. According to the authors, domestic bondmarket deregulation and opening will facilitate and increase cross-border financial transactions in Asia. As domestic residents are allowed to hold foreign bonds and foreign borrowers to issue bonds in the domestic markets, some of these domestic bondmarkets will then develop features of full-fledged international bondmarkets. Competition amongst these markets will follow and result in the emergence of regional financial centres. The role of the official sector in this approach is, in essence, to develop regional bondmarket infrastructure.

ASEAN+3 has the lead in developing regional bondmarkets in Asia. The Finance Ministers' process has established six working groups to devise plans for creating the necessary institutions' and policy cooperation among the member countries for the development of efficient Asian bondmarkets. According to Park and Park, the member countries do not adequately address an issue critical to the bondmarket development—domestic financial reform. Unless regulations on cross-border lending and borrowing are eased and removed, it is not clear whether deep and liquid bondmarkets will come into existence. If domestic bondmarkets are fortified by domestic financial infrastructure, deregulated and opened to foreign borrowers and investors, many of the Asian countries would be able to mitigate maturity and currency mismatch problems. However, it is also true that these markets will not gain competitive strength *vis-à-vis* global bondmarkets unless the countries in the region join forces to construct regional financial infrastructure. Nevertheless, Asian bondmarket development should begin with domestic financial reform.

Ito (Chapter 3) defines the objectives of Asian bonds as overcoming the problem of double mismatch, providing channels for regional saving to be directed to regional investment and reducing over-reliance on the banking system. The secondary bondmarket should be encouraged, as well as bond issues themselves. Ito proposes Asian basket currency bonds as a means to promote bondmarkets in the region. Ito points out that the Asian Bond Fund established by the Executives' Meeting of East Asia and Pacific Central Banks group in June 2003, does not achieve these objectives. The Asian Bond Fund invests in dollar-denominated bonds issued by Asian governments and institutions, which does not resolve the double mismatch problem. It also adopts a 'buy and hold' strategy so that the secondary market will not be stimulated. Central banks, using foreign reserves, would have a problem investing in corporate bonds. Therefore, channelling funds to corporations would not be achieved. Asian basket currency bonds issued against a collection of individual local-currency denominated bonds may be attractive to regional investors, overcoming informational asymmetry between issuers and investors.

Ito (Chapter 3) and Park and Park (Chapter 2) differ on issues related to the development of Asian bondmarkets, for example, on the significance of regional bias in portfolio preferences of Asian investors. Ito argues that there must be a natural preference among investors to purchase familiar products with less perceived risk. Home bias—investors from the United States holding too many American, dollar-based securities compared to the 'theoretically' calculated weight of the portfolio—is a well documented concept in finance literature. Ito thinks that Asians may prefer regional securities to domestic securities, considering the increasing familiarity with regional affairs and economic integration.

On the other hand, Park and Park argue that given non-transparency of corporate governance, unreliable accounting and auditing, and unreliability of corporate and even banking data, Asian investors may not have any informational advantage in buying Asian bonds. Park and Park focus instead on portfolio diversification. Several empirical studies have shown that most East Asian countries have displayed similar business cycles and share similar structural characteristics, which have in turn resulted in a high correlation of country risks in East Asia. As such, Asian investors cannot sensibly diversify by buying only Asian bonds. Capital account liberalisation has also increased opportunities for Asian investors to acquire more non-Asian bonds than before.

This argument is supported by the available data. The finance industry believes that a substantial portion of US dollar-denominated Asian bonds are bought and held by the investors of the issuing countries; cross-border holdings of these bonds in Asia are relatively small—there is home bias. However this home bias does not indicate the existence of regional bias. There is evidence of weak regional bias, as Park and Park demonstrate, in that the share of Asian bonds in the Japanese investors' portfolio decreased from 2.8 per cent in 1996 to 1.4 per cent in 2002. During the same period the share of Latin American issues more than doubled from 8.2 per cent to 20.3 per cent.

Some of the little evidence there is for regional bias is shown in McCauley et al. (2002) who found that 46 per cent (or 44 per cent in weighted average) of new issues in Asian securities between 1999 and 2001 (71 bonds) had been initially allocated to Asia.

Park and Park point out that even when buyers at the initial offering of bonds are mostly Asian, the final buyers may be non-Asians. Eichengreen and Park (2004) also question whether there is anything more to the Asian bid than home country investors buying dollar bonds. So, the data presented by McCauley et al. (2002) cannot be regarded as evidence of the existence of regional bias.

Regional bias, in the spirit of home bias, is still a theoretical concept. To those promoting market development, the apparent lack of evidence in investors' portfolios suggests the potential opportunity for Asian bonds and identifies the importance of regulatory obstacles.

Chapters 2 and 3 also differ on the role of the official sector in fostering Asian bondmarkets. Many advocates of Asian bonds, including Ito, think that the role of government in promoting Asian bonds is important. For example, it is important for market development that the government issues local-currency denominated bonds that are foreign-investor friendly, so that corporate bonds can be issued. Government cooperation is vital in harmonising regulatory and taxation regimes. In order to jump from bad equilibrium (a lack of investors causes no incentives to issue bonds; no bond issues causes a lack of interest among investors) to good equilibrium (deep regional markets; where issuers and investors meet), the role of government is enormous.

Park and Park propose that the role of the government be limited. They contrast a market-led strategy and a government-led strategy, and argue for the former. They also think that governments in the region will not be able to cooperate. However, market-led and government-led approaches in Park and Park are rather complementary. Making domestic markets deep and efficient is obviously very important. It is true that the government cannot do what the market will not, and the government cannot make the market buy where investors are not interested. The government should not push bonds that cannot be sold in the domestic market to foreigners. The wider the investor base, the deeper the market becomes.

The current lack of cooperation among governments may not mean that the government-led strategy is bound to fail or is inherently undesirable. Advocates of Asian bonds think that cooperation will come in the future. Some proponents have more optimistic assessments, precisely because they see benefits from success. In contrast, Park and Park point to the lack of cooperation for the expansion of the Chiang Mai Initiative among the ASEAN+3 members for the past four years as evidence of their assessment. The difference between Park and Park and Ito on this front reflects differences in judgment.

A third issue on which the two chapters put forward different views is related to whether Asian bondmarkets will help prevent future crises and whether they can change the current pattern of capital flows.

Ito supports the widely held view that a large share of long-term bonds denominated in local currencies in a country's foreign debt could reduce its vulnerability to financial crises. For instance, countries with deep and liquid bondmarkets, open to foreign investors, will ward off financial crises better than those without. The main reason for this benefit is two-fold: having long-term financing as opposed to short-term financing, and having local currency liability rather than foreign currency liability. When a crisis hits one company/sector/region in one country, it is less likely to trigger a liquidity crisis to other companies/sectors/regions/countries. It is less likely to have a crisis contagion and a crisis spiral. A crisis (sharp depreciation/a burst of a bubble) causes panic, and panic causes liquidity crisis, and then the liquidity crisis deepens and broadens. It should be stressed that this reasoning does not depend on the behaviour of investors. Investors, Asian as well as others, may dump securities anyway, but the maturities are long and rollovers are less often, so that issuers will not be subject to acute liquidity shortage.

In contrast, Park and Park propose that the argument for less probable panic rests on misunderstandings and misconceptions.

> There is a widespread presumption that the existence of well-developed regional bondmarkets in Asia would tend to reduce the share of foreign assets denominated either in the US dollar or the euro in East Asian, foreign reserve portfolios, and hence Asian savings, will remain in Asia to finance investment in the region. This presumption reflects the misunderstanding of the determinants of inter-regional capital flows between Asia and the rest of the world. There is also the misconception that well-developed Asian bondmarkets will be less susceptible to external shocks, as the majority of market participants will be Asian investors and borrowers...
>
> Knowing that their withdrawal could set off a crisis and victimise themselves, Asian investors, unlike investors from outside of the region, will be more calculating in pulling their investments out of the region. The proponents of the Asian Bond Markets Initiative suggest that prudence in risk management and possibly regional altruism will help stabilise inter-regional as well as intra-regional capital movements, thereby setting up a sturdy shield against financial crisis and speculative currency attacks (Park and Park, Chapter 2:28–29).

What Park and Park are arguing is that it is inconceivable that individual investors think as a result of collective action, and collude, explicitly and implicitly, among themselves. Ito agrees that collusive behaviour, or regional altruism, should not be a base for promoting Asian bonds. But Ito claims that the proponents do not use the argument of 'regional altruism' as the basis of their argument. Instead, according to Ito, the advocates of Asian bonds promote Asian bondmarkets because they will reduce the probabilities of a crisis as they help overcome double mismatch and reduce reliance on banking.

Park and Park question whether deep and liquid Asian local currency bondmarkets help reduce vulnerability of East Asian countries to financial crises. First of all, susceptibility to crises depends more on economic fundamentals and efficient macroeconomic management, and not so much on the availability of long-term finance. When a financial crisis occurs, it is reasonable to assume that the reserves held in short-term assets such as Treasury bills will evaporate quickly; no new international financing including trade credits from either the short or long-term end of financial markets will be available; and outstanding long-term bonds will be degraded to junk-bond status. The country in question faces a foreign exchange liquidity crisis. Foreign creditors know that foreign reserves will soon be depleted as they are used paying for imports. These developments then force creditors to demand repayment as soon as their foreign currency-denominated obligations mature.

Park and Park also point out that the idea that Asian bondmarkets açt as a buffer against financial crises is yet to be proven. If the currency mismatch in financing is as serious a problem as claimed, then Park and Park argue that Asian countries should develop and open their domestic bondmarkets before creating regional bondmarkets in Asia. There are also empirical studies showing that bank-based financial systems are no more likely to be susceptible to crises than market-based financial systems.

To substantiate their point, Park and Park consider a case where regional bondmarkets are as competitive as global bondmarkets. Then a question arises as to why those Asian borrowers who cannot issue local currency bonds in global bondmarkets will be able to do so in regional markets. What are the characteristics of Asian regional bondmarkets that can accommodate regional currency financing? The existence of regional bias, which is not evident, cannot be the answer.

Furthermore, the investor base of regional bondmarkets will be global. This means that substantial amounts of Asian currency bonds, issued in Asian bondmarkets, are likely to be held by non-Asian investors. Many exotic currency bonds (mainly central and eastern European) are issued and traded in the euro bondmarket including South African rand issues, whereas few of Asian currency bonds are issued. Why do Asian issuers not issue local currency bonds in global bondmarkets? Part of the answer lies in government regulation.

Park and Park think that having Asian bonds will not change the basic patterns of global flows of capital.

> In fact, the construction of regional bondmarkets will not change to any great degree the pattern of inter-regional capital flows in East Asia in which East Asian countries import mostly safe capital from and export risky capital to the United States and Europe...The increase in the diversity and depth of Asian bondmarkets will not necessarily increase the share of Asian bonds in the aggregate East Asian asset portfolio as long as East Asia remains a capital exporting region (Park and Park, Chapter 2:29).

Theoretically speaking, Park and Park's argument in terms of 'net' flows is correct. However, the argument has to be slightly different when we consider 'gross' flows. It is true that given current account surpluses, East Asian economies will remain capital exporters. However, Ito argues that 'gross' capital flows, currency denomination and maturity structure matter in crisis vulnerability.

Ito provides, as an example, a difference between 'net' and 'gross' capital flows. Let us consider the two cases: Asians export US$2 trillion capital and receive US$1 trillion capital; and Asians export US$1 trillion capital and receive no gross capital. In both cases, the net amount of exports is the same, US$1 trillion. In the first case, the following crisis scenario is possible. Suppose that non-Asian investors hold short-term dollar securities of, or loans to, Asian corporations. Moreover, suppose that gross capital exports from Asia were in terms of long-term investment, while gross capital imports from the rest of the world were in terms of short-term investment (dollar-denominated short-term bank loans).

Then a withdrawal of capital by non-Asians means refusing rollovers, causing a severe dollar liquidity shortage, and spilling over from corporations to banks to central banks. This is a mechanism by which even net capital exporters may fall into currency crisis. In the extreme case, Asian investors may not have to accept gross capital inflows at all, as in the second case. Then, Asian investors may not have to be subject to a sudden change in mood of non-Asian investors.

Park and Park agree that countries can run surpluses in both the current and capital accounts, and these surpluses have been added to East Asia's foreign exchange reserves, although such surpluses cannot be sustained for a long period. However, they disagree with the argument that Asian bondmarkets will reduce Asian borrowers' short-term capital imports from abroad. Even if Asian borrowers were able to issue Asian currency bonds in Asian bondmarkets, it is quite possible that non-Asians could hold substantial amounts of these Asian bonds. Furthermore, there is no evidence suggesting that Asian borrowers will be able to raise long-term funds in Asian bondmarkets, or that will not be able to in global bondmarkets. Park and Park emphasise that even Ito's extreme case of zero capital import does not shield the economy from the crisis. It is quite possible that domestic investors may start fleeing the countries when they see an impending crisis, causing a foreign exchange liquidity crisis.

At present, Asian central banks 'import' large amounts of safe US assets, as they are liquid and mostly risk-free. American and European investors also buy substantial amounts of risky Asian securities, whereas cross-border holdings of Asian securities in Asia are small. Why are Asians not buying the Asian securities that American and European investors are willing to buy? That Asian bondmarkets will change the current pattern of Asian investors' portfolio behaviour has yet to be proven.

Moreover, practically all of East Asia's holdings of short-term Treasury bills are held in reserves. Given the need to diversify country risk, it is unlikely that Asian central banks can increase substantially the share of their holdings of Asian domestic currency bonds. Well-developed domestic bondmarkets could reduce the amount of imported capital, but regional bondmarkets may not, to the extent that they have the market structure and operations similar to those of global bondmarkets.

The investor base of Asian bondmarkets will be global. It will not make much difference whether Asians or non-Asians hold Asian long-term bonds. If a country fails to manage its economy properly so that it runs a large budget and current account deficit, exposing itself as a target of speculative attack, then a large share of long-term financing will not provide much comfort.

Ito does not use the gross capital flow argument for promoting Asian bonds. He acknowledges that while this argument is commonly heard, it is superseded by other more important arguments.

On currency basket bonds, Park and Park point out there are some practical problems that could make Asian basket currency bonds less attractive to investors.

Park and Park argue that Asian basket currency bonds are basically mutual funds with fixed portfolio weights investing in bonds with different currency denominations. As such, investors cannot adjust their portfolio weights even when the prospect of currency returns change. Even if investors prefer fixed portfolio weights, the optimal portfolio weight may differ with the base currency of the investor. It is impossible to create an Asian basket currency bond with weights that would satisfy investors with different base currencies. In response, Ito states that Asian basket currency bonds may still serve as a benchmark for a basket of Asian bonds, although they may not precisely match the optimal basket of many investors. Individual investors add or subtract particular Asian bonds in addition to a base holding of Asian basket currency bonds.

Park and Park argue that if a particular currency bond included in the Asian basket currency bond pool becomes suspect (in terms of currency return or credit risk), one has to dispose of the whole holdings of Asian basket currency bonds; in mutual funds it suffices to dispose of the suspect bond alone, saving on transaction costs. Ito states that this is a valid criticism, highlighting investors' concerns, and pointing to the possible unattractiveness of Asian basket currency bonds. According to Ito, this is why the basket should consist of bonds with the same, high credit rating. Park and Park think that in this case, it would not matter whether one holds Asian basket currency bonds or individual Asian bonds.

Park and Park argue that as far as diversification of currency and credit risks are concerned, the benefits of holding Asian basket currency bonds are not likely to be higher than those of holding a portfolio of individual country bonds. Asian currencies are highly correlated to one another and credit risks of Asian bonds also show a high degree of correlation due to synchronisation of business cycles of Asian countries. If Asian bonds are highly correlated in terms of currency and credit risks, it will not make much difference whether one invests in an Asian currency basket or in any single Asian country bond. Ito points out that correlations among Asian currencies tend to vary from period to period, and even if currency risk was as highly correlated, investors would prefer to diversify to minimise credit and political risks. Mutual funds in the United States invest in various State and municipal bonds, although the 'currencies' of the States or municipality are perfectly correlated with the federal currency, the US dollar.

Park and Park observe that Asian basket currency bonds are like structured notes, requiring financial engineering techniques to calculate the theoretical value, making them unattractive even to institutional investors. The calculation becomes more complicated as the number of currencies increases. This is why European currency unit bonds were not very successful; Asian basket currency bonds present an even larger problem. Unlike European currency unit bonds, each Asian basket currency bond has a different currency and credit composition, making investors calculate their value one by one. In senior/subordinated tranching in Asian basket currency–asset-backed security bonds, rating the senior bonds must be a nightmare for credit-rating agencies let alone credit-enhancement agencies. However, Ito thinks that given information and technological sophistication, theoretical values of multi-currency bonds could be easily calculated, and currency risks easily understood. Park and Park argue that no currency basket bond in history has ever been successful.

Ito acknowledges that if full diversification is optimal for investors and if that is what investors practise, then highly correlated currencies will not be demanded. However, the home bias proves that real world investors are not full diversifiers.

Park and Park believe that the idea of Asian basket currency bonds or currency basket bonds have potential benefits, especially when the structure is simple. For example, Asian basket currency bonds with government bonds from two countries with the same or similar credit rating. Ito's position is more inclusive, arguing for bonds of several countries to be put into the basket. The difference between the two views is judgmental—the proof will come with time.

Issues surrounding Asian bonds

The remaining chapters deal with credit enhancement and securitisation in helping to develop Asian bonds. In order for Asian bondmarkets to flourish, issuers have to find it less costly to issue bonds than alternative means of financing, while investors have to find bonds worth investing in. If credit rating is not available, investors become sceptical. A regional credit-rating company, or a network of credit-rating companies, will be desirable for regional investors. Even when credit rating is available, if ratings are low, investors will not be attracted to bonds. This is the view taken by Wong and Ho (Chapter 4). They consider credit enhancement as key to Asian bond developments. This view is reiterated by Rhee (Chapter 5), Tran and Roldos (Chapter 6) and Rhee and Stone (Chapter 7). Securitisation is emphasised by Wong and Ho (Chapter 4) and Tran and Roldos (Chapter 6).

Wong and Ho discuss the challenges of promoting corporate bond issues in Asia. They focus on the issue of credit rating. The authors argue, after examining recent issues, that corporate bonds in the region are typically rated below investment grade, and are not attractive to potential issuers and global investors.

For example, at the current credit rating, Asian corporations would be required to pay an 8 per cent spread over the US Treasury bonds. This would make borrowing costs much higher than the interest rate of bank loans. Therefore, it is important that the credit rating of Asian corporations be upgraded.

Taking US municipal bonds as an example, the authors argue that an AAA-rated insurer can enhance the credit of corporate bonds in Asia. Wong and Ho argue that credit insurers can reduce or spread risk by 'overcollateralisation, diversification, reinsurance, securitisation and other techniques... A top-ranked bank can guarantee an Asian corporate bond by requesting collateral from the bond issuer for the guarantee provided' (Wong and Ho, Chapter 4:103). The authors cite the benefits of such an arrangement as follows

- bond issuers can raise funds directly from the capital market
- bond issuers can build their reputation over time
- insured bonds are marketable

- insured bonds can help the development of the market
- banks can diversify risk of concentration of bank lending to a small number of sectors/companies.

Securitisation is a good way to increase the variety and quantity of high-quality bonds. Collateralised loan obligation and collateralised bond obligation are identified as good sources of increasing the volume of high-quality securities. Korea has introduced a primary collateralised bond obligation guarantee program, with the Korea Credit Guarantee Fund. The Mortgage Corporation in Hong Kong SAR is another example. In the United States, residential mortgage loans are securitised through government-sponsored mortgage corporations. Wong and Ho propose to establish asset-backed security corporations with the support of Asian governments in dealing with bond and loan securitisation. On the investors' side, the authors propose that the government establish mutual funds to invest in the portfolio of Asian corporate debts. A model is the Hong Kong Monetary Authority's purchase of equities in 1998 to avert a financial crisis in Hong Kong SAR.

Wong and Ho identify the following steps to promote corporate issues: credit ratings should be enhanced; securitisation should be promoted; and Asian bond funds should be encouraged. They argue that promoting credit insurers is key to building an industry of credit enhancement. They refer to credit insurers in the United States, that is, to private-sector actions. Developing institutions in re-insurance and the credit derivative market is key to spreading credit risks. Wong and Ho argue that credit insurers with related financial products will make corporate bonds in the region investment-grade. Another way to transform Asian corporate bonds is asset securitisation. A move to establish corporations to securitise assets—'asset-backed security corporations'—is proposed. The asset-backed security corporations will standardise contracts and procedure, moving assets into asset pools. Then a transparent, investment-grade asset-backed security market will be born. A third way to promote corporate bonds is taken by investors. The first step is for the government to set up an Asian bond fund for Asian corporate bonds, and then to securitise government bond funds and create mutual funds that are sold to individuals and institutional investors. The Asian corporate bond fund will invest in investment-grade bonds—credit enhanced bonds—so that investors will not bear excessive risk.

Rhee (Chapter 5) describes the structure of bondmarkets in East Asia and recent movements toward building regional bondmarkets. Several bondmarkets in the region, such as Samurai bonds, Shogun bonds and Dragon bonds, are reviewed. Rhee first argues that Asians are increasingly issuing and purchasing debts in the Singaporean market, citing the evidence of

McCauley and pointing out numbers of issues in onshore Singapore-dollar denominated bonds and the offshore Asian dollar market in Singapore. For the Singapore-dollar market, a total of 27 per cent of the issuers were from the Asia Pacific region, and the majority of foreign borrowers were from the United States. Most of the Singapore-dollar denominated debts were purchased by onshore Singaporean investors. In the offshore Asian dollar market, at least 40 per cent of the borrowers were financial institutions and corporations from the Asia Pacific region.

Rhee goes on to argue that using only a portion of foreign reserves might help the development of corporate bonds in the region—namely the recycling of funds. Rhee views the importance of regional bonds as stemming from credit enhancement and the Asian common currency. Rhee points out that the New Miyazawa Initiative, which was introduced by Japan to help Asian countries in the midst of credit crunch, had an element of credit enhancement, that is, the guarantee of Asian sovereign and quasi-sovereign bonds by the Japanese government. Rhee has a vision that a common currency in Asia would increase the regional bondmarket, just as the introduction of the euro integrated the European bondmarkets with reduction in the spread.

Tran and Roldos (Chapter 6) emphasise securitisation and credit guarantees. They also summarise measures needed to lay foundations for market infrastructure and legal framework. The authors review the history of legal change to enhance securitisation: Korea passed the Asset Backed Security Law in 1998; Thailand passed the Securitisation Law in 1997; and Malaysia created the National Mortgage Corporation in 1986. Credit enhancement is also identified as a good way to broaden investor bases.

According to Tran and Roldos, improving corporate governance and transparency, including accounting and auditing standards are identified as a high-priority measure for market infrastructure. Also establishing common financial disclosure and registration rules for bond issuers is important. Standardisation of bond contracts, underwriting standards, and clearing and settlement procedure are steps toward regional bondmarkets.

Tran and Roldos identify six areas of potential policy action and reform needed to strengthen the bondmarket. First, market infrastructure has to be laid out; improving corporate governance and transparency belongs to this category. Second, a legal framework has to be established; this is most important for securitisation. It is also important to establish bankruptcy law and foreclosure practices. Third, repo markets should be developed to add liquidity to the secondary market. Fourth, derivative markets should be developed. Fifth, allowing mutual funds and pension funds to invest in corporate bonds, and inviting foreign investors by gradually dismantling capital controls should broaden investor bases. Sixth, protection of creditors' rights and rating requirements will enhance transparency. The authors take lessons from pension reform and the establishment of a local credit rating agency in Chile that contributed the development of their bondmarket.

Rhee and Stone (Chapter 7) propose region-wide credit enhancement programs. They review studies on municipal bond banks in the United States. The municipal bond banks first appeared in Canada in 1956 and in the United States in 1970. The municipal bond banks enhance credit by pooling multiple municipalities issues into a single bond bank debt issuance. By pooling bonds, credit-rating associated with the debt is changed. Municipal bond banks must have a strong credit rating to benefit from pooling bonds. Municipal bond banks can issue a large amount so that issues can be competitive. Municipal bond banks have helped municipalities without imposing financial burdens upon taxpayers.

Based on their research on the municipal bond bank model used in the United States and other western countries, Rhee and Stone believe that an application of this model to Asia could greatly help development of Asian bonds by reducing costs for the issuers and making it more attractive to investors.

This book is the first of its kind, providing a focused, in-depth examination of Asian bonds. While discussion in the chapters may overlap slightly, the different approaches taken up by the authors collectively provides a comprehensive view of Asian bonds. If all the recommendations scattered in these chapters are taken, Asia's move toward having robust financial markets is ensured.

2 Creating regional bondmarkets in East Asia

Yung-Chul Park and Daekeun Park

Of all probable structural weaknesses, the absence of vibrant bondmarkets never fails to make the long list of the causes of the 1997–98 East Asian financial crisis. A year after the financial crisis, Donald Tsang, financial secretary of Hong Kong SAR, cited the failure to establish a strong and robust Asian bondmarket as one of the reasons for the financial turmoil in East Asia, asking 'how is it that we in Asia have never been able to replicate the Eurobond market success in this part of the world?'(Tsang 1998). International financial institutions such as the International Monetary Fund (IMF) and the World Bank invariably pointed to the absence of efficient domestic bondmarkets as one of the major causes of the 1997–98 financial crisis (Independent Evaluation Office, IMF 2003). Even before the crisis, East Asian countries were urged to develop domestic bondmarkets to complement their bank-denominated financial systems.

After the crisis, the development of local bondmarkets has been highlighted as one of the major objectives of financial reforms proposed by the IMF, World Bank and Asian Development Bank (ADB) for East Asian economies. Parallel to reform efforts, there have been repeated calls for the establishment of regional bondmarkets in East Asia (Bergsten and Park 2002). Responding to these calls, and as the part of the regional efforts towards financial cooperation and integration through the Chiang Mai Initiative, the ASEAN+3 have taken steps to explore possibilities and modalities of creating Asian bonds and market infrastructures.

There is a growing interest in regional bondmarkets in East Asia in the literature. Several strategies for the creation of new, and the expansion of existing, regional bondmarkets in East Asia have been put forward. However, despite these proposals on the need for regional bondmarkets, there is little agreement on what these Asian bondmarkets are and, if there is, whether they are needed in East Asia.

This chapter analyses the rationale and strategies for creating regional bondmarkets in East Asia, looking at the characteristics of the regional bondmarkets that are likely to evolve as the region continues with financial liberalisation. It examines the role and efficiency of existing regional bondmarkets in East Asia and discusses the economic rationale and need for improving the existing, or establishing new, East Asian bondmarkets.

Asian bonds and Asian bondmarkets

An 'Asian bond' is one which is issued by governments, corporations or financial institutions of East Asia, offered for sale in a number of countries and denominated in a currency foreign to a majority of investors. An Asian bondmarket is where Asian bonds are issued and traded. Although the suppliers of these bonds are mostly borrowers from East Asia, buyers include global, as well as regional, investors. Because of this global investor base, Asian bondmarkets will not be geographically segmented markets, rather, they will inevitably be linked up with global bondmarkets.

At this stage of financial liberalisation, few of East Asia's emerging market and developing economies are prepared to issue bonds denominated in their own currency in global and regional bondmarkets. There is hesitation in allowing non-residents to hold large amounts of local currency for fear that such currency internationalisation could erode domestic control over monetary policy. Bond issues in East Asian regional markets would therefore be denominated in major international currencies such as the US dollar, yen, euro and some of the currencies of the East Asian countries, with domestic bondmarkets open to foreign borrowers such as Hong Kong SAR and Singapore.

It is widely expected that the Asian Bond Markets Initiative launched by the ASEAN+3 will spearhead the development of both domestic and regional bondmarkets in East Asia. At the regional level, the cooperative efforts of the 13 countries may set in motion three interrelated market developments for bond financing in East Asia: financial integration in the region, the emergence of regional trading centres for Asian bonds, and growth in the number of offshore regional bondmarkets. Financial integration in the region will establish closer linkages among domestic bondmarkets of individual East Asian countries. Assuming that financial reform for free and open financial markets is sustained throughout the region, and that ASEAN+3 can cooperate to construct a regional clearing and settlement system, domestic bondmarkets of individual East Asian countries will be integrated with one another to create a large regional bondmarket.

This process will be be slow, uneven and subject to the political and economic cohesiveness of the ASEAN+3, lacking at present. As shown by the European experience, even in a common currency area derailment of financial integration can occur unless market distortions are removed and market practises in different countries are harmonised. The evolution of a regionally integrated market in East Asia is at present a long-term prospect that is at best uncertain.

Regional trading centres for Asian bonds will emerge as a number of individual countries open their bondmarkets to foreign borrowers and investors. Japan, Hong Kong SAR, China, Singapore and Korea all have plans for transforming their domestic bondmarkets into international or regional bondmarkets. The bonds issued by foreign entities in these markets will be denominated in the currencies of these prospective regional financial centres. Therefore, a number of Asian bondmarkets, differentiated by the currency denomination, are likely to come into existence, such as the yen, Singapore dollar and Hong Kong dollar markets.

Along with the growth of these onshore international bondmarkets, a number of offshore regional bondmarkets, similar in structural characteristics to the old Eurobond market, will emerge as new sources of bond financing in East Asia. Several offshore regional bondmarkets already exist, and these and new offshore markets may gain deeper and more liquid features as financial market deregulation and opening permeate throughout East Asia. Bonds issued in these markets are likely to be denominated in major international currencies, some of the currencies of East Asian countries with open domestic bondmarkets. Issuance of Asian bonds in these offshore bondmarkets is likely to consist of private placements offered by underwriters via dealers to institutional and private investors. Offshore bondmarkets will be subject to little regulation from host regulators and withholding income taxes. Disclosure may also depend on the prominence of the issuance and will be less stringent than the onshore markets, increasing the speed of issuance. These characteristics constitute the source of competitive advantage in these markets.

Some of the bonds issued in these offshore markets will be listed in regional financial centres because the listing tends to improve the liquidity, and hence the marketability, of a bond, although most Asian bonds are likely to be registered securities and traded in the over-the-counter market. The onshore domestic bondmarkets open to foreign borrowers and offshore regional bondmarkets are separate but interdependent markets. Over time the increase in institutional investors in the region, and competition between them, will lead to convergence of the two markets.

Several countries in East Asia have been active in regionalising or internationalising their domestic bondmarkets and also in hosting offshore regional bondmarkets. At this stage, it is not clear which countries will survive the ongoing competition to emerge as major trading centres for Asian bonds. In view of the European experience, it appears that countries with deregulated and open financial markets and with an efficient system of payment and settlement will succeed over other competitors as East Asia's major regional trading centres for Asian bonds.

Efficiency of Asian bondmarkets—both onshore and offshore—will hinge on developed regional systems of payment, clearing, settlement and depository services that ensure real time gross settlement with delivery versus payment for cross-border transactions of bonds. Depth and liquidity of Asian bondmarkets will also improve if regionally specialised rating agencies are established.

At present, the requisite infrastructure for regional bondmarkets hardly exists and it may take years to establish. If prospects for the Asian Bond Markets Initiative are promising, some countries aspiring to be regional financial centres will take the lead in constructing region-wide financial infrastructures. Cooperative efforts at the regional level for integrating different local clearing and settlement systems in different countries are needed but, in the absence of official sector intervention, may not be organised easily and may not succeed even if they are organised. However, the competition for hosting regional bondmarkets, together with the Asian Bond Markets Initiative of the ASEAN+3, may bring the economies in East Asia together to build a regional financial infrastructure.

Regional bondmarkets in East Asia

The current debates on, and numerous proposals for, creating Asian bondmarkets may give the impression that East Asia has no regional bondmarket where regional entities can raise capital by issuing bonds denominated in East Asian currencies. In fact, there are already a number of offshore and onshore regional bondmarkets located in Tokyo, Hong Kong SAR and Singapore that are accessible to East Asian borrowers.

Most of these markets have not served as important sources of financing to a majority of East Asian borrowers as they have a relatively small investor base. Largely because of high issuing costs, East Asian borrowers who can issue bonds in global bondmarkets have ignored these markets.

Tokyo has two offshore bondmarkets—the Samurai bondmarket where foreign borrowers can issue yen-denominated bonds and the Shogun bondmarket open to foreigners to issue bonds denominated in foreign currencies (Appendix 2.1). In Hong Kong SAR, foreign borrowers receive the national treatment and can issue bonds as freely as Hong Kong SAR residents in its domestic bondmarket. In 2002, the Central Moneymarkets Unit was established to facilitate settlement, clearing and depositary services related to secondary market trading of these international bonds.

Singapore has an offshore Asian dollar bondmarket where most of the issues are denominated in US dollars (92 per cent in 2001). Singapore has also deregulated its domestic corporate bondmarket to allow foreign borrowers to issue Singapore dollar-denominated bonds since 1998 (Appendix 2.2).[1] Between the opening of the domestic Singapore dollar market to foreign issuers in August 1998 and to the end of 2002, S$10.3 billion bonds were issued by foreign entities in Singapore dollars (Ngiam and Loh 2002). Because of the currency trading restriction (designed to discourage the formation of an offshore Singapore dollar market) foreign issuers must convert their proceeds into a foreign currency when they are taken out of the country. This restriction has limited the scope of the Singapore domestic bondmarket as a regional market.

Financial deregulation has also increased the opportunities for cross-border bond financing and trading in Korea. For example, the Korean authorities have deregulated many capital market activities so that foreign borrowers can issue bonds denominated not only in the Korean won but also in other currencies. Deregulation is yet to attract many foreign borrowers: the number and amount of foreign issues have been negligible. As in Singapore, the won proceeds have to be converted into a foreign currency when they are taken out of the country because of the policy of not allowing internationalisation of the won.

The issuer base is also small for both onshore and offshore regional bondmarkets in East Asia; fiscal prudence in the region has limited the supply of sovereign bonds. The supply of corporate bonds in these markets has been even smaller, largely because bank financing has been relatively cheaper than bond financing and the number of corporations that can obtain an investment-grade rating has been small.

Tokyo has been a logical candidate for the trading centre of an Asian bondmarket given its size and the potential of the yen as a major international currency. The city has yet to serve as a centre, because it has failed to build the efficient institutional infrastructure required for bond issuing and trading. The prospects for internationalising the yen also do not appear to be promising (Park 2002).

The cost of raising funds on Asian bondmarkets is likely to be higher than in global bondmarkets, as evidenced by recent developments in the Japanese

Samurai and Shogun bondmarkets. Although it is expected that foreign borrowers would take advantage of the low interest rates and continuing deflation in Japan, the issuance of Samurai bonds amounted to only 3.8 trillion yen in 2002, less than one tenth of the pre-crisis peak level (38.7 trillion yen) in 1996, while no Shogun bonds have been issued since 1994. One of the most important reasons for this inactivity is simply the higher cost of borrowing through these markets than the Eurobond market or the Yankee bondmarket. Rhee (2001) shows that the difference in all-in-cost to a sovereign borrower of 20 billion yen between the Samurai and euro–yen bonds is about 7 basis points (14 million yen). The lead time required from mandate to launch takes a few days in the euro–yen issue, whereas it takes two to three months in the Samurai bond issue. Foreign issuers are also subject to a cumbersome regulation that requires a Japanese prospectus.

Inefficiency of the clearing and settlement process is another reason for the high cost of borrowing through the Samurai bondmarket. The transactions of euro–yen bonds can be settled through international central securities depositories, such as Euroclear and Clearstream, whereas the Samurai bondmarket is not eligible for such global clearing and settlement. Growth of the Tokyo markets has also been hampered by the lack of a regional clearing network in East Asia that links Tokyo's clearing system with the region's financial centres such as Hong Kong SAR and Singapore.

The rationale for creating Asian bondmarkets

Since the 1997–98 crisis, there has been a growing regional movement toward financial and monetary integration in East Asia. The Chiang Mai Initiative reflects such regional efforts for integration. Policymakers of the ASEAN+3 have also been working on developing a blue print for the creation of Asian bondmarkets as part of their strategy for expanding the scope of financial cooperation and deepening economic integration among the member countries.

Over the past five years, total savings of ASEAN+3 on an annual average have accounted for 19.7 per cent of global savings, larger in an absolute amount than those of the European Union. More than 12 per cent of these savings has been lent to the United States and other parts of the world to finance their investment. Collectively, the region has sustained a much higher savings rate than both Europe and North America. The combined GDP of the 13 countries was equivalent to 20.7 per cent of world GDP in 2002. These macroeconomic indicators leave little doubt that the region has an economic capacity in terms of savings and investment to support large and efficient capital markets.

Despite the large economic base, both domestic and regional bondmarkets are underdeveloped and hardly serve as a major source of investment financing. There are a number of reasons for the absence of efficient bondmarkets in East Asia. East Asia has not nurtured a market-oriented financial culture as its financial system has long been dominated by banks and other financial intermediaries. In many countries, small and medium-sized firms are not creditworthy in the eyes of the institutional investors who constitute the majority of bondmarket investors. On the other hand, large firms with global exposure and investment-grade ratings have migrated to global bondmarkets. The region could have at least supported markets for high yield East Asian bonds with speculative credit ratings. As shown by Wong and Ho (2003), there has been little demand for Asian high yield bonds as they are not as attractive in terms of the risk-adjusted returns as similar US corporate bonds to most regional and global investors. Most of the East Asian countries have therefore neglected, or put off, strengthening financial infrastructures required for broad and deep bondmarkets, and have had little incentive to train and develop the skilled personnel who move the markets—dealers, traders, investment bankers and portfolio managers.

Since 1998, most of the countries in the region have set the development of bondmarkets as their financial reform priority with the realisation that a balanced financial system, in terms of markets and financial intermediaries, is key to maintaining financial stability. As the fear of another financial crisis has receded, so has the initial resolve for financial reform. The Asian Bond Markets Initiative, it is often argued, will sustain financial reform, thereby helping East Asian countries achieve their reform objectives.

In contemplating the creation of regional bondmarkets, East Asian policymakers will be asking three fundamental questions regarding the benefit and cost of building regional bondmarkets and requisite financial infrastructures. One question is whether East Asia needs, and can support, regional bondmarkets. If it does, then another question is whether these markets can become efficient in terms of the cost of borrowing to survive competition *vis-à-vis* global bondmarkets. Would they grow into robust and liquid markets to improve capital allocation, to open new and more investment opportunities than before, and to contribute to financial stability and integration in East Asia? Finally, what could East Asian policymakers collectively do to assist launching and developing regional bondmarkets in the region?

At this stage of development, there is no guarantee that regional bond initiatives mounted by the ASEAN+3 could succeed in fostering regional capital markets that are as competitive as global capital markets in North America and Europe. With continuing globalisation of financial markets and advances in financial technology that allow financial firms in international financial centres to reach investors and borrowers in remote corners of the world, questions also arise as to the need and rationale for creating regional capital markets in East Asia.

Efficiency gains

Given its dynamism and the availability of a large pool of savings, many argue that East Asia could support large and efficient regional bondmarkets, which can be as competitive as global bondmarkets. If these markets can be created and made competitive, then East Asian borrowers will benefit from the greater availability of funds, possibly at a lower cost than before. On the demand side, East Asian institutional and private investors would gain from deep and liquid regional bondmarkets as a greater variety of bond instruments could facilitate management and improve the risk-return profiles of their asset portfolios.

While potential benefits from broad and deep regional markets could be substantial in terms of efficiency gains, these benefits would be greater if regional markets were fully integrated with global markets. If global financial integration is the ultimate objective of financial market opening, then it may follow that East Asian countries would be better off by integrating domestic bondmarkets with global ones from the beginning rather than creating and integrating with regional bondmarkets.

With greater access to better and more reliable information on the activities of individual corporations, in both developed and developing economies, institutional and private investors from East Asia and other parts of the world have increasingly sought out investment vehicles from different regions and countries to diversify the risks of their portfolio investments. Financial market opening and deregulation of capital account transactions throughout the global economy have also dissipated regional, as well as domestic, bias in portfolio investment. As East Asian economies open their financial markets, a growing number of firms will respond to international capital markets as they meet the requirements for cross-listing on, and capital raising from, international exchanges (Eichengreen and Park 2003).

Efficiency gains do not necessarily provide the economic rationale for creating Asian bondmarkets in a world economy where financial markets are increasingly globalised; East Asia could benefit more from global integration. However, many developing economies in East Asia simply do not have domestic bondmarkets, with prospects for developing them unpromising. Except for those of Singapore, Hong Kong SAR and Tokyo, most bondmarkets in East Asia are shallow and narrow so that they cannot be integrated into global bondmarkets. At the same time, there is dissatisfaction with global bondmarkets with the sentiment that they are discriminating against Asian bond issuers because they tend to ignore Asian firms with high credit quality and good growth prospects. If these concerns are valid then East Asian policymakers can build a strong case for their Asian Bond Markets Initiative on the grounds that regional markets will serve as a new source of bond financing to many East Asian firms, and in doing so build a *bloc* for the global integration of bondmarkets in the long run.

Promoting financial stability

Sudden reversal of capital flows to the five East Asian crisis countries, leading up to the financial crisis—Indonesia, Korea, Malaysia, Philippines and Thailand—was on the order of US$105–110 billion. Before the crisis, many governments could not issue sovereign bonds in global bondmarkets and the number of corporations that could was limited in East Asia. In the absence of domestic bondmarkets, much foreign lending took the form of short-term bank loans denominated in US dollars. As a result, foreign debts of these countries consisted mostly of short-term dollar denominated obligations. At the end of 1996, China, Hong Kong SAR, Japan, Singapore and Chinese Taipei held a combined total of US$700 billion in foreign reserves, much of which was invested in short-term dollar-denominated assets. Restoring financial stability in Indonesia, Korea and Thailand required the IMF to mobilise a total of US$59.7 billion from various sources, including its own facilities for the liquidity support for the three countries.

These figures clearly demonstrate that an allocation of 10 per cent of the foreign reserves of the five non-crisis East Asian economies to the crisis countries for liquidity support could have averted or at least mitigated the severity of the crisis. At that time, East Asia as a whole held a large amount of liquidity in the form of reserves, but the region did not have either market or official sector cooperative mechanisms that could have lent some of these reserves to countries experiencing capital account crises.

According to Rhee (2000), deep and liquid domestic and regional bondmarkets could have provided market-oriented mechanisms to overcome crises. In the absence of well-developed regional bondmarkets, however, a large portion of foreign exchange reserves of East Asian countries was held in US dollars or European currency-denominated assets. The bulk of these were then recycled back to East Asia in the form of short-term bank loans denominated in US dollars, in the absence of efficient domestic bondmarkets. This pattern of capital flows—importation of safe assets and exportation of short-term risky assets—made the region vulnerable to speculative attacks before the crisis. This pattern has changed little since the 1997–98 crisis. Despite their large holdings of foreign exchange reserves, East Asian economies are still exposed to a high probability of the recurrence of financial crises.

Since the crisis, most East Asian countries have turned from net capital importers to net capital exporters, as they have amassed large amounts of current account surpluses, much of which has been added to their foreign exchange reserves. As a result, total reserve holdings of 13 East Asian economies amounted to US$1.2 trillion at the end of 2001 (Table 2.1 and Table 2.2). Most of these reserves have been invested in safe and liquid assets such as US Treasury bonds and supranational bonds with relatively low yields. At the same time, East Asian borrowers still rely heavily on short-term bank loans for their foreign financing, paying high risk premiums.

There is no denying that the development of domestic bondmarkets in East Asia should be accorded a high priority on the financial reform agenda as it will contribute to stability and efficiency in the financial sector. However, it should be noted that the existence of a well-developed domestic bondmarket does not necessarily prevent or reduce the severity of a financial crisis. It is also incorrect to argue that the existence of deep and liquid domestic and regional bondmarkets can keep domestic savings and foreign reserves in the region, which in turn can be channelled to financing investment of East Asian corporations or can provide the region with a protective shield against speculative attacks and financial crises.

Domestic bondmarkets and financial stability

As has been argued by many, including Krugman (1998) and Aghion, Bacchetta and Banerjee (2001), the 1997–98 East Asian crisis can be characterised as a twin crisis where a speculative attack on the currency, aggravated by a squeeze on bank liquidity, developed into a full-blown economic crisis. In fact, incentive distortions in the bank-dominated financial system were at the bottom of the East Asian crisis. Implicit government guarantees on bank deposits and use of banks as an instrument of industrial policy had bred the moral hazard syndrome of over-borrowing and over-investment before the crisis. Once the crisis unfolded, many bank loans became non-performing.

In these bank-dominated economies, banks also served as the main channel through which foreign banks and non-bank financial institutions lent to local borrowers in East Asia. Once the amount of non-performing loans started ballooning and the fear of currency depreciation set in, foreign lenders began cutting off credit lines and refusing to rollover their short-term loans to the

East Asian banks. When the banks were unable to service their foreign currency loans, they became insolvent, precipitating a major financial crisis. The banking crisis proved to be even more devastating than otherwise thought—the firms that had depended on bank loans could not find alternative sources of financing.

Many observers argue that had there been efficient domestic bondmarkets, investors' locked-in bonds (both domestic and foreign) could not have left East Asia as hurriedly as they did. Institutional investors, who constitute the majority of buyers of sovereign as well as corporate bonds, tend to hold bonds in their portfolios until maturity. In particular, they will not sell bonds they hold if they are going to incur large capital losses. Even if they sell the bonds, some other investors will have to hold them until maturity. This means that the reversal of capital flows would be relatively small and the depletion of foreign reserves would be equally small even when financial panic sets in.

When the prospects for East Asian economies were as bleak as they were at the beginning of the crisis, it is hard to believe that investors would have held on to the bonds in their portfolios, knowing that their capital losses would mount with the deepening of the crisis.

When a liquidity crisis occurs, it is reasonable to assume that much of reserves would evaporate very quickly, no new international financing including trade credits from short or long-term financial markets would be available, and long-term bonds outstanding would be degraded to a junk-bond status. Foreign creditors, knowing that foreign reserves would deplete as soon they paid for imports, would demand repayment as soon as their foreign-currency denominated obligations matured. If a country is known to suffer from an insolvency crisis, then the share of long-term bonds in its total foreign debt will not make much difference in preventing the crisis.

A recent report by the International Monetary Fund's Independent Evaluation Office (2003) argues that the underdevelopment and closedness of bond and short-term money markets exacerbated the 1997–98 crisis. The absence of the long-term bondmarket, and the short-term money market, open to foreign investors meant that high interest rate policy would not be effective in arresting the decline in the exchange rate and stabilising the market. Foreign entities did not have many investment instruments through which to invest in local currency-denominated assets. Therefore, a policy of higher interest rates could not stabilise the local currency by increasing the cost of speculation against them, given that there was no evidence that speculators were taking large short positions in the local currency.

The crisis-hit countries were facing increased demand for liquidation of foreign currency claims rather than a speculative currency attack at the

Table 2.1 **Foreign reserve holdings in East Asia, 1993–2002** (US$ billion)

	1993	1994	1995	1996	1997	1998	1999	2000	2001	2002
China	22.39	52.91	75.38	107.00	142.70	149.10	157.70	168.20	215.60	286.41
Indonesia	11.26	12.13	13.71	18.25	16.59	22.71	26.45	28.50	27.25	31.57
Korea	20.23	25.64	32.68	34.04	20.37	51.97	73.99	96.13	102.70	120.81
Malaysia	27.25	25.42	23.77	27.01	20.79	25.56	30.59	29.52	30.47	34.58
Philippines	4.68	6.02	6.37	10.03	7.27	9.23	13.23	13.05	13.44	16.06
Singapore	48.36	58.18	68.70	76.85	71.29	74.93	76.84	80.13	75.37	81.37
Thailand	24.47	29.33	35.98	37.73	26.18	28.83	34.06	32.02	32.35	38.92
Hong Kong SAR	42.99	49.25	55.40	63.81	92.80	89.65	96.24	107.50	111.10	..
Japan	98.52	125.80	183.20	216.60	219.6	215.40	286.90	354.90	395.10	451.46

Source: International Monetary Fund, *International Financial Statistics*, International Monetary Fund, Washington, DC.

Table 2.2 **Shares of East Asian reserve holdings in world, 1993–2001** (US$ billion)

	1993	1994	1995	1996	1997	1998	1999	2000	2001
Total reserves in Asia		412.20	520.70	617.90	649.30	701.90	837.50	957.00	1,061.21
Total reserves in World	994.10	1,142.80	1,361.80	1,537.70	1,602.10	1,651.20	1,975.80	2,105.80	2,201.10
Reserves in Asia/World (%)	31.73	36.07	38.23	40.19	40.53	42.51	42.39	45.45	48.21

Source: International Monetary Fund, *International Financial Statistics*, International Monetary Fund, Washington, DC.

beginning of the financial crisis. At the height of the crisis, however, it was not clear whether any level of interest rates offered by East Asian borrowers would have been high enough to induce foreign banks to roll over their loans. In view of the preceding argument, it is difficult to lay the blame for the crisis entirely on the absence of open local bondmarkets.

Regional bondmarkets: exporting risky assets and importing safe assets

There is a widespread presumption that the existence of well-developed regional bondmarkets in Asia would tend to reduce the share of foreign assets denominated either in the US dollar or the euro in East Asian, foreign reserve portfolios, and hence Asian savings, will remain in Asia to finance investment in the region. This presumption reflects the misunderstanding of the determinants of inter-regional capital flows between Asia and the rest of the world. There is also the misconception that well-developed Asian bondmarkets will be less susceptible to external shocks, as the majority of market participants will be Asian investors and borrowers.

If regional bondmarkets can exist in East Asia, it is possible that East Asian investors will hold a larger proportion of Asian bonds than their foreign counterparts. The predominance of regional investors in Asian bondmarkets may then have different implications for stability of financial markets in the region.

Since participants in Asian bondmarkets have access to better (and more) information on the economic policies of individual countries for the region's corporations, it is conceivable that they would be less prone than investors from outside the region to irrational panic and bank-run syndrome in managing their investments. The market participants would also be better positioned to identify 'unsound' firms and to differentiate systematic from non-systematic risks. If most of the risky East Asian securities are held by investors from the region, then one could argue that the degree of reversal in capital flows would tend to be smaller in a crisis situation. This improvement in the quality and quantity of market information for portfolio investment in regional bond instruments will then help ward off contagion of a financial crisis and moderate volatility in financial prices in the region. While this may be true in theory, the evidence does not support differences in behaviour between Asian and European or American investors.

Knowing that their withdrawal could set off a crisis and victimise themselves, Asian investors, unlike investors from outside of the region, will be more calculating in pulling their investments out of the region. The proponents of the Asian Bond Markets Initiative suggest that prudence in risk management and possibly regional altruism will help stabilise inter-regional as well as intra-regional capital movements, thereby setting up a sturdy shield against financial crisis and speculative currency attacks. It is an open qualification whether Asian investors are less inclined to speculate on Asian bonds, equities and foreign exchange than western investors.

However, the experience with the 1997–98 crisis does not necessarily support this argument. Suppose that there existed an Asian yen bondmarket before the crisis. Would such a market have prevented a crisis or made the consequences of such a crisis less painful? It would not have, because investors in both regional and global markets are likely to have the same pattern of behaviour as far as their credit risk management is concerned. In fact, there is little difference in terms of the demand for bonds between the Asian yen and other global bondmarkets in that investors in these markets buy only high quality investment-grade bonds. A large amount of bond financing relative to bank financing could have made East Asian economies less vulnerable to speculative attacks, but it is not clear whether the size of the Asian yen bondmarket would have made any difference in lessening financial vulnerability of the region.

If indeed access to better and more country-specific, as well as firm-specific, information is as important as claimed, East Asian investors should have been much more restrained than investors from outside the region in withdrawing their investments during the 1997–98 financial crisis. In particular, it was widely held that the crisis-hit countries suffered a liquidity, not an insolvency, crisis. This was not the case. Indeed, the lending behaviour of Japanese banks was hardly different from that of western banks during the crisis period, so the argument based on differences in the quality of information accessible to regional and western investors does not necessarily hold.

In fact, the construction of regional bondmarkets will not change the pattern of inter-regional capital flows in East Asia in which East Asian economies import mostly safe capital from, and export risky capital to, the United States and Europe. In any given year, change in the total amount of bonds and other securities issued by US and European corporations and government that are held by East Asian governments in the form of foreign reserves and also by private investors is largely determined by macroeconomic conditions governing current account developments in East Asia, the United States and Europe. As long as East Asia as a whole continues to run current account surpluses as it has in the past, in particular *vis-à-vis* the United States, then either the government or the private sector in Asia is bound to accumulate US and European securities. An increase in the diversity and depth of Asian bondmarkets will not necessarily increase the share of Asian bonds in the aggregate East Asian asset portfolio, as long as East Asia remains a capital exporting region.

An increase in the supply of Asian bonds, in particular East Asian sovereign and high-quality private bonds, and the expansion of the secondary markets for these instruments could over time reduce the share of US dollar and euro-denominated securities in the foreign reserves of East Asian countries. However, as long as the current account imbalances between East Asia and the rest of the world persist, a decrease in the share of US and European securities in the reserve portfolios will be made up for by an equal increase in private holdings of these securities.

Regional bias in portfolio investment

Regional bias in portfolio investment, if it is pronounced, may provide justification for creating Asian bondmarkets. Although there is dearth of information, it is reasonable to assume that East Asian governments, corporations and individual savers have taken advantage of capital market liberalisation to place in part their funds in bonds and equities issued by East Asian borrowers with which they are familiar. McCauley, Fung and Gadanecz (2002), for instance, show that the aggregate amount of bonds issued by East Asian borrowers over the three-year period from April 1999 to August 2002 amounted to US$41.2 billion; East Asian investors then bought up 46 per cent of these primary issues. East Asian governments and government agencies issued more than 40 per cent of these bonds.

McCauley et al. present the East Asian share of the primary market distribution as evidence of a relatively high degree of integration among East Asian capital markets. Crockett (2002) makes a similar argument. In gathering these data, McCauley et al. admit, 'we solely rely on second-hand reports from underwriters that are at best approximation' (2002:84).

Aside from their quality, we believe their data could not identify the final buyers of these East Asian bonds. It is quite possible that East Asian financial institutions, as well as subsidiaries of foreign investment banks, purchased the bonds and brokerage houses located in Hong Kong SAR, Singapore and Tokyo and purchased the bonds for their investors from America and Europe. It is in general difficult to ascertain whether residents in one country buy bonds issued by the entities in their own country or whether they buy bonds issued by borrowers in other countries.[2]

However, there is a piece of evidence that casts doubt as to the ownership composition of McCauley et al. (2002). Japan—the largest exporter of capital of the world—has acquired more Latin American bonds than Asian bonds in recent years. In 1996, the share of Asian bonds in the total overseas portfolio investment of Japan was 3.2 per cent as opposed to 8.3 per cent for Latin

Table 2.3 **Foreign holdings of Korean securities, 1999–2002** (hundred million won)

	Market capitalisation		Foreign holdings		Ratio of foreign holdings(%)	
	Stock	Bond	Stock	Bond	Stock	Bond
1999	3,495,039	3,644,186	765,905	11,567	21.9	0.31
2000	1,880,414	4,236,835	565,585	6,921	30.1	0.16
2001	2,558,500	5,047,298	936,982	4,293	36.6	0.09
2002	2,586,807	5,639,436	931,607	6,466	36.0	0.11

Source: Financial Supervisory Service, Korea.

America; by 2001, the Asian proportion fell to 1.3 per cent (14.1 per cent for Latin American bonds). Between 1999 and 2001, Japanese holdings of Asian bonds fell by 250 billion yen (US$200 million) (Table 2.3).

Questions then arise as to the identity of those investors from East Asian economies who invested in 46 per cent of primary issues of East Asian paper between 1999 and 2002 as claimed by McCauley et al. (2002). Since investors from East Asian countries, including Japan, have expressed a preference for safe assets, it is difficult to believe that residents of Hong Kong SAR, Singapore and Korea bought more East Asian bonds than Japanese investors during the same period.

Crockett (2002) argues that East Asia has been importing safe assets while exporting risky ones. Foreign direct investment, portfolio equity, bad loans and bonds are risky East Asian assets acquired by American and European investors. East Asian investors, on the other hand, have been importing low risk securities such as US Treasury bonds, US agency paper and interbank deposits. If East Asia has been importing safe assets and there has been a limited variety and quantity of safe bonds issued by East Asian borrowers, then it is difficult to accept the data provided by McCauley et al. (2002) or Crockett's argument that among the buyers of East Asian bonds, East Asian accounts take almost half of the issues which are relatively more risky assets than US bonds.

In general, foreign reserves are held in safe and liquid assets. Much of the increase in East Asia's holdings of safe foreign assets corresponds to the massive increase in its foreign reserves. East Asian institutional investors have been relatively more risk averse than their US and European counterparts largely because they have not developed or acquired sophisticated risk management technologies and have limited access to information about global, as well as regional, borrowers. Many of the financial institutions of East Asian emerging market economies became highly vulnerable to financial crisis, and some of them went bankrupt, as a consequence of the poor risk management of their asset portfolios, leading to large investments in risky bonds issued by other emerging market economies' borrowers. The lessons of the 1997–98 crisis and the subsequent tightening of regulations on assets management have made East Asian investors more conservative in managing risk of their asset portfolios, but they may have a long way to go before reaching the global standard of risk management.

This aversion to risk is seen in the large increase in East Asia's demand for US government and government agency bonds in recent years and reduced share of Asian securities in the Japanese aggregate investment portfolio. While the percentage of East Asian equities and bonds in the Japanese aggregate portfolio declined substantially, the share of capital market instruments issued by US and European entities rose to 90 per cent of total foreign assets held by Japan in 2000 and 2001.

Asian bondmarkets: complementary to global bondmarkets

International bondmarkets, such as the Yankee and Eurobond markets, are not readily accessible to most East Asian borrowers because of their low credit ratings. In order to issue bonds in international bondmarkets, issuers need to get investment-grade ratings from international credit-rating agencies. Most institutional investors in these markets, including pension and investment funds, are operating under the mandate that, to be included in their portfolio, bond issues must be rated by international credit-rating agencies and that they must have investment grades. Only a limited number of East Asian corporate issuers have been able to obtain investment grades from international credit-rating agencies, although investment-grade ratings can be obtained from domestic rating agencies.

There is usually a large gap between ratings on domestic corporations acquired from domestic credit-rating agencies and their international foreign currency ratings acquired from global credit-rating agencies. This gap originates in the bias that international foreign currency ratings are restricted by the sovereign ratings of the countries where the corporations are located. In general, sovereign issuers get the highest credit rating (AAA or its equivalent) when domestic currency bonds are rated by local credit-rating agencies. However, international bonds denominated in foreign currencies are usually given lower credit ratings. Many East Asian government issues, excluding those of Hong Kong SAR, Japan and Singapore, belong to the sub-investment grades or the lower range of the investment grades. This means that their corporate issuers are likely to belong to the sub-investment grades when rated by international credit-rating agencies, which in turn means that they do not have independent access to international bondmarkets.

The Yankee and other foreign bondmarkets impose even stricter disclosure rules and public offering requirements than the Eurobond market. Most Asian corporate issuers do not have access to the Samurai bondmarket under the current regulation. As a result, there is certainly a case for regional bondmarkets if these markets can accommodate bond financing of some of East Asian local issuers with low or no credit ratings with attractive costs.

Asian bondmarkets could be structured to accommodate many Asian corporate bonds with a medium grade or belonging to the upper range of the sub-investment grades such as BBB, BB and B, thereby making them complementary to global bondmarkets. Once these markets for bonds denominated in key regional currencies are established, it is also expected that regional financial derivative markets for currency swaps and options will come into existence to facilitate the issuance of bonds denominated in the local currency for many East Asian emerging market economies. The development of these markets will then help ease the currency mismatch problem.[3]

The regional Bond Markets Initiative promoted by the ASEAN+3 could reduce the credit quality gap as it will encourage creation of regional credit-rating agencies specialised in rating East Asian corporate issuers. This regional specialisation may uncover more creditworthy regional borrowers than global rating agencies because regional agencies will be better informed about regional economies, social and political developments and have more resources to gather and analyse firm specific information resulting in regional ratings having to rely less on the sovereign ratings of the economies where these East Asian firms are domiciled.

Asian bondmarkets could also provide an opportunity for cross-border bond financing to smaller East Asian countries with underdeveloped financial sectors. Except for Japan and China, smaller East Asian countries may find it difficult to develop domestic bondmarkets that are broad and deep in terms of the variety of instruments available and market participants, since these economies are relatively small in size.

Asian bondmarkets may support large capital markets with scale economies and cost competitiveness. The costs of constructing financial and other institutional infrastructures required for supporting domestic bondmarkets could be prohibitively expensive to many emerging market and developing economies in the region. Unless local bondmarkets are competitive in terms of the cost of borrowing, local borrowers would avoid bondmarket financing in favour of bank financing. Sovereign, as well as corporate, borrowers from these financially underdeveloped countries have little or no access to global bondmarkets.

The regional initiative for the creation of Asian bondmarkets could contribute to the development of more balanced financial systems with efficient bondmarkets in East Asia in two ways. The growing competition among the East Asian countries to host as regional bond trading centres will generate incentives for them to deregulate and open domestic bondmarkets to increase the investor base and liquidity of these markets.

Other countries may also remove restrictions on bond financing and capital account transactions so that their residents could take advantage of regional bondmarkets as an additional source of financing. For those smaller economies with underdeveloped financial systems, regional bondmarkets could serve as substitute for domestic bondmarkets.

A critical evaluation

Several proposals have been made regarding the strategies for, and modalities of, creating Asian bonds and Asian bondmarkets (Chaipravat, Supapol and Sangsubhan 2003, Ito 2003, Oh and Park 2003). These proposals are designed to alleviate the two mismatch problems: the maturity mismatch and the currency mismatch that have plagued East Asian corporations and financial institutions.

All of these proposals advocate the use of structured financing, like securitisation, as a means to overcome the maturity mismatch problem. In order to further increase the marketability of Asian bonds, the use of credit enhancement mechanisms such as credit guarantees and the establishment of the Asian Bond Bank are also recommended. Ito (2003) and Chaipravat et al. (2003) propose the issuance of currency basket bonds to overcome the currency mismatch problem. Oh and Park (2003) argue that the development of currency swap arrangements would be a better strategy to enable East Asian borrowers to raise funds in their own local currency. The following section evaluates these proposals.

Narrowing the maturity and credit quality gap

Since the maturity mismatch problem arises mainly from the credit quality gap, it can be resolved by enhancing the credit quality of the securities to the level acceptable to investors. The credit quality gap could in turn be reduced through structured financing schemes like securitisation, and credit enhancement and credit guarantee.

Securitisation

Securitisation is a form of structured financing in which securities are issued through repackaging a series of assets that generate cash flows in a way that separates these assets from the credit profile of the company that originally owned them. Securitisation can take on a large variety of attributes depending on the structure, underlying assets, the way underlying assets are managed and the types of securities issued.

Potential benefits of securitisation include cost efficient funding, credit risk mitigation, diversification of funding sources, tenor and currency management. In the majority of cases, the real motivation for securitisation is more likely to be risk mitigation and de-leveraging of the balance sheet at the cheapest cost rather than just access to cheap funding.

Securitisation is useful in resolving the maturity mismatch problem in several ways. The true sale nature of the securitisation deal allows the creditworthiness of the asset-backed securities to be independent of the creditworthiness of the company that originally owned the underlying assets. The credit assessment of asset-backed securities is made solely on the basis of the cash flows created by the underlying assets. In addition, securitisation schemes such as collateralised bond obligations and collateralised loan obligations can reduce the overall credit risk of the pool of collateralised bonds by diversifying the idiosyncratic credit risk of each borrower. This coinsurance effect from pooling debt instruments, issued by companies with different risk profiles, enables the collateralised bond obligation scheme to raise more funds than the sum of the funds each company can raise by itself.

Despite the benefits from credit risk diversification and coinsurance, securitisation by itself cannot remove the credit risk of underlying securities. Instead, it enables the issuers to sell the credit risk at a lower cost. It reduces the overall cost of raising funds by creating securities whose credit risk profile is tailored to the risk preferences of the customers. In particular, bonds with a higher credit rating than the underlying assets can be issued by using the senior/subordinate tranches. Generally, senior bonds can receive credit ratings higher than the collateralised assets, and hence can be absorbed by the corporate bondmarket.

In addition to senior/subordinate tranching, other credit enhancement methods such as over-collateralisation, spread accounts, cash collateral accounts, credit swaps and credit guarantees can be used to enhance the creditworthiness of the asset-backed securities and make them attractive to even a greater range of investors.

An example of the use of securitisation to promote Asian bondmarkets is the two-tier securitisation scheme for financing small and medium enterprises

Figure 2.1 **Two-tier securitisation scheme for small and medium enterprise financing**

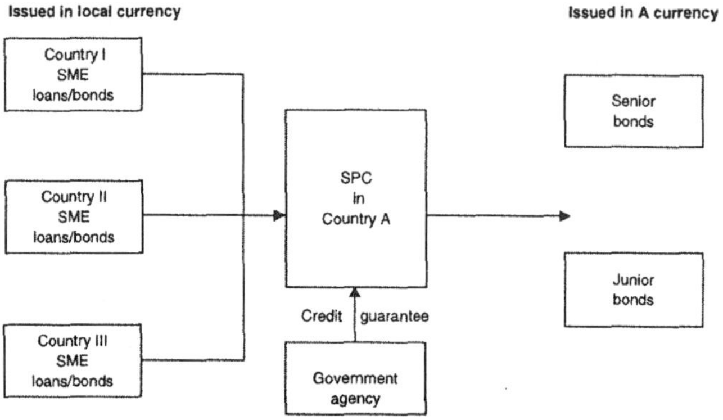

Source: Oh, G. and Park, J., 2003. Fostering Asian bond markets using securitization and credit guarantee, presentation at the Voluntary Working Group Meeting on the Asian Bond Markets Initiative, Tokyo, 16 June.

suggested by Oh and Park (2003). This securitisation scheme consists of two steps of the securitisation process: the first step in each of capital importing countries and the second in the capital exporting country (Figure 2.1).

In the first step, a local special purpose company is set up in each of the capital importing countries to securitise small and medium enterprises loans or bonds. The loans and bonds to be collateralised may be denominated in the local currency in order to eliminate the currency mismatch problem. In order to minimise the problem of moral hazard, the junior tranche bonds will be assumed by local institutions that are in charge of selecting the firms to be included in the collateralised loan obligation or collateralised bond obligation pool. The senior tranche bonds are sold in the local bondmarkets and the remainder will be transferred to the second special purpose company established in the capital exporting country. The senior tranche bonds may be guaranteed by the local credit guarantee agency to increase their marketability.

In the second step of the securitisation, the special purpose company established in the capital-exporting country-issues collateralised bond obligations using the senior bonds it acquired from the special purpose companies located in capital importing countries. Once again, different tranches of bonds will be issued to better fit the preferences of investors. In order to further enhance creditworthiness and marketability, the senior tranche bonds may acquire credit guarantees.

The securities issued by the special purpose company can be denominated in one of the international vehicle currencies, in the currency of the capital abundant East Asian country, or in the basket currency unit. The list of underlying assets can be expanded to government bonds, non-performing assets and corporate bonds.

There are, however, a few stumbling blocks in using securitisation schemes to develop Asian bondmarkets. One barrier is that the legal framework facilitating securitisation differs widely among East Asian economies. World Bank (2002) recognises wide differences in the legal framework regarding securitisation. For example, while the common practice of Hong Kong SAR, Singapore and Malaysia to acknowledge trusts already provides the institutional foundation required for securitisation, civil law countries need to enact the securitisation law that recognises the pass-through status of the special purpose companies and the true sale nature. Another barrier is the different accounting standards and tax treatments for special purpose companies in different countries. With the exception of Japan, Korea, Hong Kong SAR and Singapore, issuers and investors are not familiar with securitisation schemes. Availability of previous records or historical data is also an important factor for the success of securitisation deals.

Credit guarantees

Many Asian bonds are likely to belong to the junk bond category by the standard of the international bondmarket. A large number of East Asian firms do not have credit ratings good enough to issue bonds in the domestic bondmarket let alone international bondmarkets. As a result, even in the securitisation scheme, the amount of funds that can be raised through senior bonds is likely to be quite limited. In order to increase the portion of securities that can be absorbed by the market, credit guarantees can be utilised. Credit guarantees on timely payment of interest and principal enhance the creditworthiness of bond issues because issues with a full credit guarantee can acquire the credit rating of the guarantee agency. Credit guarantee agencies may provide coverage for the entire issue or a specific tranche.

Credit guarantees can be obtained from private credit guarantee agencies like mono-line insurance companies and multi-line insurance companies, government agencies and international financial institutions. However, the existing credit guarantee agencies may not be suitable for providing credit guarantees for regional bonds. For example, the Japan Bank for International Cooperation (JBIC) cannot provide credit guarantees on corporations or special purpose companies. The JBIC can only guarantee bonds denominated in the Japanese yen. The Asian Development Bank and the JBIC are restricted from providing guarantees to bonds issuers from advanced economies. As a result, regional securitisation deals involving issuers from Japan or Korea cannot obtain credit guarantee services from these official sector agencies.

Private credit guarantee agencies in general prefer dealing with credit risk alone and as a result are reluctant to provide currency swaps together with credit guarantees while more effective schemes for regional bonds may require currency swaps to overcome the currency mismatch problem in addition to credit guarantees. Private guarantee agencies might also have limited capacity to provide guarantees.

In order to provide credit guarantee services for Asian bondmarkets more efficiently, it would be useful to establish an international organisation to provide regional credit guarantees. The operational mode (mono-line or multi-line) and the governance structure (an international agency or a private company) need to be discussed and negotiated. The regional guarantee agency may also provide currency swaps.

Resolving the currency mismatch

Depending on the types of bonds and market arrangements to be created, regional bondmarkets could assist issuers to overcome the currency mismatch problem, although they will not provide a solution. This section evaluates proposals for resolving the problem of currency mismatch in the context of regional bondmarkets.

Currency basket bonds

Chaipravat et al. (2003) and Ito (2003c) propose issuance of currency basket bonds as a way to overcome the currency mismatch problem. For example, Asian basket currency (ABC) bonds as suggested by Ito are constructed as bonds backed by a mix of local currency government bonds issued by East Asian countries. The value of the ABC bonds will therefore be determined by the weighted value of the currencies comprising the basket.

While, in theory, currency basket bonds could moderate the currency mismatch problem, it is not clear that international investors are willing to hold such bonds. Currency basket bonds might be acceptable to international investors as they help to diversify currency risks. The size of the benefit from diversification depends on the degree of correlation among the underlying currencies. East Asian currencies tend to be positively correlated with each other, suggesting that the diversification effect of the currency baskets comprising East Asian currencies alone might not be large enough to attract investors (Table 2.4). Moreover, the correlation between the East Asian currencies increases in times of turbulence like the 1997–98 East Asian crisis due to the contagion effect, further reducing the diversification benefit.[4]

Table 2.4 **Correlation between East Asian currencies**

	November 1995–June 2003						
	KRW	IDR	MYR	PHP	SGD	TWD	JPY
KRW		-	-	-	-	-	-
IDR	0.4742		-	-	-	-	-
MYR	0.4586	0.6582		-	-	-	-
PHP	0.5284	0.6494	0.7143		-	-	-
SGD	0.4703	0.6998	0.6824	0.6184		-	-
TWD	0.4774	0.4737	0.4966	0.5082	0.6231		-
JPY	0.2834	0.2323	0.2692	0.2248	0.5244	0.4819	
	January 1997–December 1998						
	KRW	IDR	MYR	PHP	SGD	TWD	JPY
KRW		-	-	-	-	-	-
IDR	0.5000		-	-	-	-	-
MYR	0.4712	0.7022		-	-	-	-
PHP	0.5672	0.7110	0.8170		-	-	-
SGD	0.5035	0.7247	0.8176	0.7555		-	-
TWD	0.4815	0.5740	0.5918	0.5462	0.7555		-
JPY	0.2153	0.3490	0.3968	0.3204	0.6043	0.5490	
	January 1999–June 2003						
	KRW	IDR	MYR	PHP	SGD	TWD	JPY
KRW		-	-	-	-	-	-
IDR	0.2337		-	-	-	-	-
MYR	0.0148	0.0332		-	-	-	-
PHP	0.3732	0.3772	0.1265		-	-	-
SGD	0.3638	0.6429	−0.0558	0.2449		-	-
TWD	0.5142	0.1502	−0.0189	0.3938	0.3378		-
JPY	0.5962	0.0581	−0.0192	0.1308	0.4760	0.4428	

Source: Authors' calculations.

In order to examine the magnitude of the diversification effect, a few examples of currency baskets comprising East Asian currencies will be constructed and their variability compared with that of the major currencies. The currency basket comprising the six East Asian currencies—the Korean won, the Chinese yuan, the Malaysian ringgit, the Thai baht, the Hong Kong dollar and the Singapore dollar—shows higher volatility than the Japanese yen (Figure 2.2). The result does not change even when additional currencies such as the Indonesian rupee, the Philippine peso and the Japanese yen are included (Table 2.5).

Another problem with the currency basket bond is that the cost of monitoring movements in several currencies may reduce the diversification

Figure 2.2 **Asian currency basket versus the Japanese yen, 1993–2002**

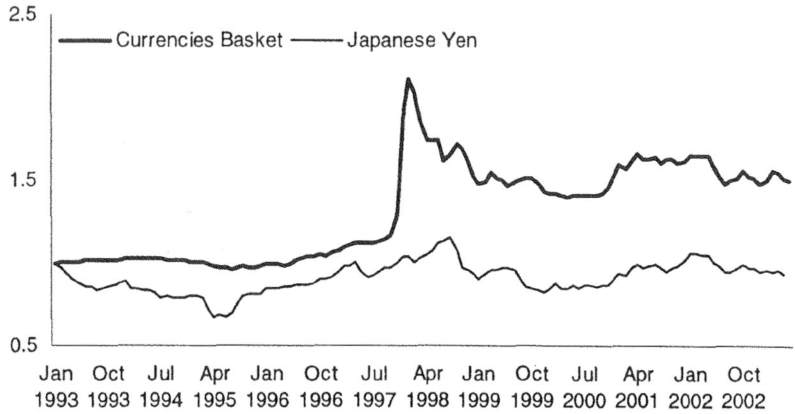

Source: Pacific Exchange Rate Service. Available online at http://fx.sauder.ubc.ca.

benefit. The high monitoring cost may be the reason why the World Bank currency pool loan was phased out and replaced by the single currency loan due to lack of demand. It also explains why ECU-denominated bonds were not very popular.

One could argue that currency speculators who expect appreciation of the currencies comprising the basket will be induced to hold the currency basket bonds. However, since the currency composition of these bonds are fixed, currency speculators cannot change the composition even when bilateral exchange rates of the underlying currencies are expected to change. In general, currency speculators are likely to prefer managing their own currency risks. This means that as far as speculators are concerned, they would prefer holding a portfolio consisting of bonds denominated in different currencies than currency basket bonds. If the Asian currency unit is widely accepted as a unit of accounting and the exchange rate policies of East Asian countries can be coordinated, then there will certainly be a larger demand for currency basket bonds.

Currency swaps

The issuance of Asian bonds denominated in a variety of East Asian local currencies will be facilitated if swap markets for these currencies are established. For those economies with a well-developed swap market, issuing bonds denominated in the local currency would be possible and cost effective. For a currency without a developed swap market, questions arise as to whether the official sector should step in to provide swap arrangements or to develop infrastructures for the swap market. The official intervention may contain an element of subsidisation to the extent that the official swap provider takes the risk of unhedged swap positions at a price below the market level. To counter this view one could argue that the underdeveloped swap market is a public good which may justify the intervention in its development.

Credit enhancement and currency tranching

Credit enhancement and securitisation could assist in removing some of the risk related to the currency mismatch in balance sheets of corporations and

Table 2.5 **Standard deviation of the rate of currency depreciation, 1993–2003**

	Jan. 1993–Jun. 2003	Jan. 1998–Jun. 2003
United Kingdom	1.760	1.666
Japan	2.889	2.843
Index[a]	4.699	2.699
China	4.466	0.009
Hong Kong SAR	0.524	0.024
Malaysia	2.820	2.167
Singapore	1.487	1.601
Korea	4.825	2.756
Thailand	3.904	2.975
	Nov. 1995–Jun. 2003	Jan. 1998–Jun. 2003
United Kingdom	1.692	1.666
Index[b]	6.768	5.207
Index[c]	3.215	2.210
China	0.040	0.009
Hong Kong SAR	0.036	0.024
Malaysia	3.188	2.167
Singapore	1.636	1.601
Korea	5.643	2.756
Thailand	4.561	2.975
Japan	2.718	2.843
India	1.184	0.795

[a] Korea, Thailand, China, Malaysia, Hong Kong SAR, Singapore.
[b] = [a] + Philippines + Japan
[c] = [b] + India
Source: Authors' calculations.

financial institutions. If the credit risk associated with currency basket bonds can be removed through credit guarantees, then investors will be more willing to hold them despite the currency risk, because the investors can then focus on managing the currency risk. Eliminating the credit risk makes it easier for investors to evaluate and price the risk they take more accurately.[5]

The use of currency tranching in securitisation may also be useful in mitigating the currency mismatch problem if there is a substantial demand for each currency tranche. Suppose that collateralised bond obligations are issued on the collateral of won and baht-denominated bonds. Three currency tranches may be created by securitisation: the yen-denominated bonds, the currency basket bonds denominated in the Korean won and the Thai baht and the bonds with claims on the remaining cash flows. Investors purchasing the third tranche bonds are taking a short position on the Japanese yen and a long position on the currency basket of the Korean won and the Thai baht. It means that the investors purchasing third tranche bonds can expect the same return on investment in bonds denominated in Korean won and the Thai baht, financed by a yen loan. When the yen appreciates against the won and the baht, the return on third tranch bonds will be low or even negative. The effectiveness of the currency tranching in resolving the currency mismatch will, in the end, depend on whether there is an enough demand for such an investment position.

Although there is no denying that the methods introduced so far have, in theory, some potential to minimise the currency mismatch problem it is doubtful that they would be effective in reality. The most effective, and realistic, way of dealing with the currency mismatch is to encourage foreigners to invest in local-currency denominated bonds in domestic bondmarkets. Therefore, improving bondmarket infrastructure and removing institutional bottlenecks to increase foreign investment in domestic bonds needs to be a priority of financial reform.

A road map for the development of regional bondmarkets

A market-led evolutionary process

The discussion so far suggests that a number of regional bondmarkets differentiated in terms of the issuing currency would emerge in the course of financial liberalisation and integration in East Asia. Several countries aspiring to be regional financial centres have already taken steps to open their domestic bondmarkets to foreign borrowers or to create an offshore market. Competition among these markets will ensue and both borrowers and investors will migrate to the markets with the most efficient payment and settlement system, thereby creating regional financial centres.

However, few Asian emerging market economies could issue bonds denominated in their own currencies while these countries do not allow non-residents to hold their currencies. It is conceivable that Asian bonds denominated in an Asian currency unit—a composite of regional currencies weighted by their relative economic importance—could be created through a regional cooperative scheme. However, it is not clear if there will be any demand for this type of bond.

In developing regional bondmarkets, East Asian countries could take either a market-led or government-led strategy. The market-led or evolutionary approach relies more on competition among the countries attempting to transform their domestic capital markets into regional markets. In this approach, the involvement of, and cooperation amongst, East Asian governments would be confined to developing financial, legal and regulatory infrastructures and harmonising the market regulation and provided at the regional level. A more direct government-led strategy requires active participation on the part of East Asian governments, in addition to building financial and other institutional infrastructures, in diversifying the menu of bondmarket instruments by issuing multiple categories of government bonds and introducing schemes of credit guarantee and enhancement, and securitisation. The official sector may also support the creation of regional rating agencies.

Although the policy authorities of Japan, Korea and Thailand have been reviewing several strategies for developing regional bondmarkets, it is not likely that they would be able to agree on any single strategy. Even if a strategy was agreed, it is not clear whether it could be implemented. Since the interests of these countries in promoting the Asian bond initiative are different and they are all competing to host a regional trading centre, negotiations for a common development strategy would be a drawn-out process. If an Asian bondmarket is to take off, Asian bonds, sovereign or corporate, will need to be tailored to the preferences of private and institutional investors in terms of maturity and credit quality. This is because at the early stage of the bondmarket's development, institutional investors, including various types of investment funds, insurance companies and investment banks, are likely to dictate what types of bonds can be issued and traded. These investors will also promote healthy competition and the construction of regional financial infrastructures.

In order to develop the regional bondmarkets, these market participants will have to be involved in the planning stages and the role of the official sector in this process will be supportive of removing impediments to market development. For these reasons, ASEAN+3 will be better advised if they follow a market-oriented approach.

If Tokyo, Hong Kong SAR and Singapore want to develop their domestic bondmarkets into regional bondmarkets, or to create offshore international bondmarkets, then it is their business to attract borrowers and investors by offering a low cost of issuance. In order to serve as a fully-fledged financial centre, these countries will have to create a variety of market-supporting institutions together with insurance and financial derivative markets. Out of necessity, they will also lead the construction of regional financial infrastructures in East Asia.

Domestic financial reform

Historical experiences show that financial development in general proceeds from simple lending and borrowing arrangements to a system dominated by commercial banking and eventually to a broader system complemented by a variety of non-bank financial institutions and money and capital markets. Thus, in most developing economies, largely because of problems related to lack of information and inefficient legal systems, capital markets for primary securities such as stocks, bonds, mortgages and commercial bills are insignificant channels for mobilising and allocating savings. Therefore, for all practical purposes, the banking system—broadly defined to include a variety of depository institutions—dominates the financial system and is usually the only organised credit market available.

Empirical studies also support this evolutionary process of financial development. According to Demirguc-Kunt and Levine (2001), national financial systems tend to become more market-oriented as countries become richer. In higher income countries, they show that financial systems are more developed, with stockmarkets becoming more active and efficient relative to banks. One plausible explanation for the evolutionary process is provided by a legal approach to the determination of financial structure and financial development. According to the legal approach, financial contracts are well defined and are effective by virtue of rights and enforcement mechanisms. Therefore, it follows that a well-functioning legal system facilitates and improves the operation of both financial institutions and markets (La Porta, Lopez-de-Silanes, Shleifer and Vishny 1999).[6] In a recent paper, Levine (2000) shows that the legal rights and effectiveness of contract enforcement is strongly associated with long-run growth: the legal system is a crucial determinant of financial development. In another empirical paper, Levine, Loayza and Beck (2000) show that the legal rights of investors, the efficiency of contract enforcement and accounting systems help to explain cross-country differences in the level of financial development.

One important implication of the legal approach to finance is that countries with a tradition of English common law tend to have market-based financial systems which stress the rights of minority stockholders. Other legal origins such as French and German civil law systems are associated with underdeveloped and bank-based systems. For example, the German system, which stresses creditors' rights to a much greater degree than other systems, generates beneficial repercussions for financial intermediary development. Countries with weak accounting standards and explicit or implicit deposit insurance systems are likely to have bank-based financial systems. Among the advanced economies, Germany and Japan have a bank-based financial system with Japan's legal system being modelled on the German system. Japan was not known for strong accounting standards (comparable to Anglo-American standards) and had not instituted a formal deposit insurance system until the early 1990s. These legal and other institutional features may explain, in part, the bank-based dominance of the Japanese financial system.

Since most of the East Asian countries, except for Japan, are either emerging markets or developing economies, this evolutionary process of financial development suggests that East Asia's financial systems were, and still are, dominated by banks and other financial intermediaries. In fact, many authors claim that East Asian financial systems that can be characterised as a bank-based system (Aoki 2000, Eichengreen and Hausmann 1999a, Park 1993). It is also widely accepted that for more than three decades preceding the 1997 crisis, most East Asian countries had relied on the banking system as instruments of industrial policy—as the means of mobilising savings and allocating them to strategic industries and favoured projects (Haggard 2000).

The bank-oriented system has largely been responsible for the lack of professional expertise, inadequacy of the financial and legal infrastructures (including regulatory systems) low standards of accounting and auditing, and non-transparency of corporate governance which all have plagued the development of capital markets in East Asia. Efficient and stable regional bondmarkets are not likely to take root unless East Asian economies speed up financial reform, strengthen financial and legal infrastructures, and introduce and enforce international standards for accounting, auditing and governance.

While one can make a case for creating regional bondmarkets in East Asia, such markets will not grow unless domestic financial reform precedes, or is carried out in parallel with, the development of Asian bondmarkets. The first step toward developing regional bondmarkets should begin with domestic financial reform to remove impediments to issuing and trading in domestic bonds and to build domestic financial infrastructures.

To many East Asian economies, regional bondmarkets will be new sources of foreign currency financing. Unless domestic financial markets and capital account transactions are liberalised, domestic lenders and borrowers will not be able to take advantage of these new sources of financing on regional bondmarkets. Without the active participation of regional investors and borrowers, robust regional bondmarkets will not take root. Region-wide financial and institutional reform will therefore be crucial to nurturing a fertile ground on which regional capital markets can grow.

Domestic financial reform is also necessary to resolve the currency mismatch problem. As noted in the preceding section, regional bondmarkets will not offer a solution to this problem; only effective and domestic bondmarkets open to foreign investors will help East Asian countries avoid the currency mismatch problems.

From the standpoint of the East Asian borrowers, issuing bonds in the regional bondmarket is just one financing option out of several possible alternatives including bank loans and equities. On bond financing alone, East Asian borrowers have access to domestic, international and regional bondmarkets. Then, the question naturally arises as to why local borrowers might prefer cross-border bond financing in East Asia.

When the borrowing cost in the domestic market rises due to an imbalance between the supply and demand for funds, it may be less expensive in terms of the cost and availability of funds to choose cross-border financing, even when the exchange rate risk and other issuing costs are taken into consideration. Imbalances in the demand for, and supply of, different categories of bonds might occur even though there is sufficient investment demand for domestic bonds as a whole. For example, changes in asset preferences such as a flight to quality in the domestic bondmarket may increase the spread on sub-investment-grade bonds. If a similar flight does not take place in international bondmarkets, then cross-border financing may be less costly. Likewise, when the supply of bonds of a particular industry or sector increases substantially, the overall amount of the idiosyncratic risk of these issues may become too large to be borne by the pool of domestic investors alone, and as a result raise their spreads disproportionately. In this case, the issuers can reduce the borrowing cost by dispersing the idiosyncratic risk to the international investor pool where the risk might not be as large as in the domestic market. This risk diversification is similar to the credit default swaps provided by foreign investors.

Nevertheless, in most East Asian economies foreign participation in the domestic bondmarket is restricted or limited for a number of reasons. Foreign investors often do not have access to these markets due to capital control problems. For example, Korea has an active domestic bondmarket, which has been open to foreign investors since 1997. Yet foreign participation in the domestic bondmarket has been minimal. Foreigners held only 0.11 per cent of total domestic bonds as of end-2002 (Table 2.1), compared to 35 per cent of the stockmarket capitalisation held by foreign investors. This indicates that the bondmarket is, in effect, closed to foreign investors. Regulatory restrictions and the lack of market supporting institutions are often cited as being responsible for the small foreign presence. Furthermore, inadequate accounting standards or practices and improper disclosure requirements have made non-transparent corporate governance of the issuers. Bankruptcy laws and procedures are not reliable. Despite the large volume of outstanding issues, the bondmarket has not been for all practical purposes liquid enough to facilitate foreign investors' bond portfolios.

Taxation is also another factor that discourages foreign investment in local bonds in East Asia. Some countries, including Korea, impose withholding taxes on interest income earned by non-residents as well as that earned by residents, whereas countries like the United States, Japan and Singapore grant non-residents exemption from withholding taxes on interest income. There is no withholding tax on Eurobonds. Despite the tax treaties that avoid double taxation, the tax withholding remains and has been a barrier to cross-border investors.

The lack of availability of hedging instruments such as currency swaps, currency options and forward contracts has also been an impediment to cross-border investors in acquiring East Asian domestic bonds. Because of the paucity of money market instruments and underdevelopment of currency swap markets, foreign investors often find it difficult to hedge against interest rate and exchange rate risks. Even if they are available, the currency swap market is so shallow that even a small change in the supply and demand causes a large swing in swap rates, which in turn may lower significantly the covered return on cross-border fixed-income investments. There are also restrictions on trading these bonds outside their country of issue, which have limited the size of the secondary markets for these bonds.

Perhaps the most serious limitation to foreign presence in East Asia local bondmarkets is that the number of firms qualified to receive an investment-grade rating from global rating agencies is very small. For instance, in Korea, the number is estimated to be less than 31 out of 188 listed corporations that have acquired domestic credit ratings between January 2002 and May 2003.[7] Since foreign investors, in particular institutional ones, have a strong preference for high quality bonds with low credit risks, the supply of Asian bonds in which foreigners can invest has been very small.

In view of the importance of, and in order to overcome the domestic opposition to, domestic financial reform faced by many of the East Asian countries, multilateral efforts at the regional level are urged to support and facilitate financial liberalisation throughout East Asia. In this regard, the Asian Bond Fund is misguided if it is designed to stimulate the supply of Asian bonds denominated in major currencies. At present, the problem with regional bondmarkets is not the lack of demand; in fact, there is already too much liquidity in these markets. Creditworthy East Asian corporations can issue bonds at low prices and the spread on East Asian corporate bonds is the lowest in the world. Only the financial and institutional reform will bring more high-quality issues into domestic bondmarkets.

The crisis-hit economies in East Asia which received rescue financing with policy conditionality have made considerable progress in reforming their financial systems. However, as the fear of another round of crises has receded and the recovery of these economies, despite the ongoing global slowdown, has been faster than expected, and the domestic opposition by the vested interests has mounted, reform efforts have slowed down and have given way to the *status quo* in these economies.

Furthermore, the two economies which could, and should, provide leadership in managing regional financial integration and cooperation, have been mired in serious banking and other financial problems themselves so that they are in no position to lead region-wide financial reform in East Asia. At present, one cannot find any serious market forces that could sustain their financial reform. East Asian governments do not appear to have either the will or the external pressure to continue with their reform efforts. Now that the crisis is over multilateral financial institutions such as the International Monetary Fund have no clear mandate to oversee reform in these countries. Many proposals for domestic bondmarket development have been made by the World Bank, the Asian Development Bank and the Asia Policy Forum, but they are largely ignored. What is unsettling is that the CMI economies have been preoccupied with Asian bonds while ignoring the need to organising a joint program for supporting financial reform in individual East Asian countries. Without reforms to domestic financial systems, there is a high probability that the Asian Bond Markets Initiative may meet the fate of past regional efforts that did not go anywhere.

Complementary bondmarkets

East Asian borrowers have the option of issuing bonds in local, regional and global bondmarkets. As noted earlier, most of the large corporations that can obtain an investment-grade rating have migrated to global bondmarkets. They also have access both to global and domestic equity markets. Many small and medium sized firms are not capable of raising capital from either local or regional bondmarkets, although some of them have a good credit record. Who will then raise funds in the regional bondmarkets in East Asia?

Given the preference of institutional investors for quality, there is not likely to be a strong demand for high-yield Asian bonds, so one cannot expect a large increase in the supply of top-grade Asian bonds in the foreseeable future. Many of the issuers who can borrow from these regional markets also have access to global bondmarkets. Since issuing costs are likely to be high at the beginning, there will be few top-grade East Asian firms utilising Asian bondmarkets. These structural constraints suggest that regional markets would have a better chance of survival if they were structured to be complementary to either domestic or global capital markets. Indeed, it would be an erroneous strategy if Asian bondmarkets attempted to lure away creditworthy East Asian borrowers from global bondmarkets.

Regional bondmarkets in East Asia cannot remain separated from global financial markets. With the opening of the financial services industry, foreign investment banks, brokers and dealers will play an important role in developing regional capital markets in East Asia, in particular in forming a critical mass of East Asian issuers and investors. Because of their dominance in supplying capital market services in global financial markets, they will also be instrumental to harnessing linkages between regional capital markets and global markets.

If the planners of the Asian Bond Markets Initiative emulate the issuing procedures, regulation and market infrastructure of global bondmarkets, Asian bondmarkets will not take off; most likely they will become as moribund as the Samurai and Shogun. Asian bondmarkets will also not be a viable source of financing if they are primarily designed to accommodate the borrowing needs of low-rated or unrated East Asian bond issuers because there will be little demand for high-risk Asian bonds.

There are a multitude of categories of bonds between top-grade low-risk bonds and high-yield high-risk bonds in global bondmarkets. The success of Asian bondmarkets will depend on identifying and bringing into the markets those issuers who do not have access to global bondmarkets but do have good credit records. To this end, the creation of regional credit-rating agencies specialised in East Asian bond issues would assume critical importance in launching and developing regional bondmarkets in East Asia.

Initially, sub-standards bonds, issued by creditworthy East Asian firms, could be made more attractive to risk-averse foreign investors through credit enhancement and guarantee of these bonds. However, credit enhancement and guarantee facilities often do not exist. Where they do exist, the cost of the credit quality improvement tends to be high, making bond financing less attractive than bank financing. High-yield bonds issued by those corporations and financial institutions with speculative grades could be then transformed into investment-grade paper through the creation of special purpose vehicles which issue and market bonds of their own, backed by the sub-standard bonds they pool together. At this stage, however, only Korea, Hong Kong SAR and Singapore have been able to utilise the asset securitisation scheme.

Regional cooperation and official sector intervention

The 'leaving it to the market' approach will be the most logical alternative for East Asian countries in the development of Asian bondmarkets. However, these markets will not simply spring up, unless the official sector intervenes to organise and initiate the launching of these markets. The Asian Bond Markets Initiative could be thwarted or distorted by the vested interests of the banking and equity market. At this stage, investment banks, investment intermediaries and other market participants do not appear to have the ability or the incentive; although they are prepared to jump once profit is assured. What would then be the scope of government involvement and what would be the specific intervention measures?

In the long term, the objectives of the official sector intervention organised by the ASEAN+3 are clear. They are

- implementation of a regional assistance program for domestic financial reform
- consolidation and integration of clearing and settlement systems of individual countries
- support for the establishment of regional credit rating agencies
- harmonisation of legal, regulatory, and tax systems.

In smaller East Asian developing economies, creating an efficient domestic bondmarket may be extremely costly and will most likely end in failure unless institutional reform of corporate governance, accounting and disclosure to protect the investors' rights are implemented. In this regard, the ASEAN+3 are urged to develop institutional arrangements, including financial, to support financial reform in these countries.

Even if a bondmarket can be created, it remains uncertain whether the market will be a competitive source of financing compared to bank and equity market financing. Smaller East Asian economies may have incentives to forgo developing domestic bondmarkets if they could depend on regional and global bondmarkets for long-term financing without encountering the currency mismatch problem. For these countries, cooperative efforts at a regional level may be directed to providing institutional support of credit, enhancement and guarantee and currency swaps to increase their access to regional bondmarkets.

One of the key issues related to the development of regional bondmarkets may be the creation of a single central securities depository in the region for safekeeping, clearance and settlements for all securities traded in the region. To obtain efficiency and stability of regional capital markets a large number of market-supporting institutions need to be created: regional credit agencies, cross-border securities borrowing and lending mechanisms, credit enhancement and guarantee agencies, clearing and settlement systems, a centralised depositary system, and exchanges and over-the-counter markets for bond trading. In addition, different financial standards, regulatory systems and tax treatments in different countries in the region need to be harmonised (Rhee 2001).

A well-organised clearing and settlement process is a critical feature of a smoothly functioning regional bondmarket, providing for the efficient transfer of ownership from the seller to the buyer. An efficient cross-border clearing and settlement requires access to systems in different countries and the interactions of different system. In East Asia, the existing infrastructures for clearing and settlement for cross-border securities transactions is rudimentary and remains highly fragmented. Since investors from East Asia and other regions are required to access many national systems with different types of services, technical requirements and with different legal and tax frameworks, the costs of cross-border transactions associated with poor infrastructure are high and a major limitation on the scope of cross-border securities trading in East Asia.

The planners of the Asian bondmarket development must first identify the existing barriers to efficient cross-border clearing and settlement in terms of national differences in technical requirements and market practices, as well as national differences in tax and legal procedures. Once these barriers are identified, it will become clear which can be addressed by the private sector and which will require official intervention.

A recent report on integration of the clearing and settlement systems in the European Union (Giovannini Group 2001, 2003), shows that the most serious barriers to integration are restrictions on settlement activities in individual countries. Removal of these restrictions is the first step that will set in motion a market-led integration of clearing and settlement activities. Among these barriers, differences in the information technology, operating hours, settlement periods, intra-day settlement finality and issuance practices can and should be harmonised by the private sector. The barriers related to taxation and legal certainty would require cooperation among the ASEAN+3 governments.

In principle, the private sector should be able to develop schemes for credit enhancement and insurance. In fact, there are many insurance companies who specialise in this business. Therefore, public sector involvement should be limited to cases of market failure, such as providing credit rating assistance to small and medium-sized firms and sovereign borrowers unable to obtain an investment-grade rating.

Ferri and Liu (2002) show that corporations in developing economies are discriminated against in credit rating by global credit-rating agencies, in that these ratings are very much bound by their sovereign ratings, regardless of their domicile. Firms in developing economies are rated low because their sovereign ratings are low, which is mostly caused by the poor quality of institutions and information disclosure.

The long-term solution to this problem is to improve the rule of law and the quality of information disclosure by investing more, or social capital and institution building. In the short-run, joint efforts by the ASEAN+3 could organise regional schemes to cooperate with global rating agencies to devise separate firm level ratings based on firm specific risks only. Ferri and Liu (2002) also propose mechanisms of credit enhancement and guarantee as a short-run measure. If private credit insurance institutions are not efficient, resulting in a majority of firms being without access to credit improvement mechanisms at reasonable prices, then one can make a case for official sector involvement. However, if government-sponsored credit-improvement institutions are managed in a loose manner, then government involvement runs the risk of creating moral hazard problems, which will interfere with financial reforms and institution building in individual countries.

Concluding remarks

Several proposals have been made regarding the strategies for, and modalities of, developing regional bondmarkets in East Asia. This paper has examined the economic rationale and need for creating regional bondmarkets from the perspectives of borrowers, as well as investors, from East Asia.

Our analysis of the prospects for creating regional bondmarkets makes it clear that the development of domestic bondmarkets should precede the development of regional bondmarkets in East Asia. Deep and liquid domestic bondmarkets could relieve many East Asian emerging market economies of the burden of the twin mismatches of maturity and currency of the balance sheets of corporations and financial institutions of these economies. Regional markets are also expected to contribute to stabilising capital flows between East Asia and the rest of the world and could serve as a potential shield against future financial crises. To many smaller developing economies in the region, however, the development of domestic bondmarkets can be so costly that they may have to rely on either regional and global bondmarkets to raise long-term capital.

For efficiency and stability, regional bondmarkets cannot remain isolated but must be linked to global bondmarkets. Countries aspiring to become regional financial centres in East Asia are expected to develop efficient market infrastructures and a free market environment to attract regional issuers and investors to their markets. Through competition, some of these countries will emerge as major regional financial centres. At this stage of development, some of the most important cooperative tasks facing the ASEAN+3 are to encourage and sustain domestic financial reform in the member countries and to build regional financial infrastructures to facilitate robust and efficient regional bondmarkets.

Notes

1 Monetary Authority of Singapore Notice 757.

2 The authors owe this point to Charles Adams of the International Monetary Fund.

3 The 'original sin' problem is not confined to East Asian borrowers. It applies to all developing economies. Bond issuance in international bondmarkets is dominated by five international vehicle currencies including the US dollar, the euro, the Japanese yen, the Swiss franc and the pound sterling. The international debt securities denominated in these five major currencies explain more than 97 per cent of the total international debt securities outstanding as of the third quarter of 2002. According to Eichengreen, Hausmann and Panizza (2002), of the nearly US$5.8 trillion in outstanding securities placed in international markets in the period 1999–2001, US$5.6 trillion was issued in these five major currencies. Of the US$1.3 trillion debt issued by international organisations and by residents of countries other than the countries issuing these five major currencies, only US$0.2 trillion debt was denominated in currencies other than these five currencies.

4 Eichengreen et al. (2002) show that the real exchange rate based currency basket comprising 20 international currencies, including East Asian currencies has shown stability even during the 1997–98 East Asian currency crisis.

5 Eichengreen et al. (2002) argue that this is one of the reasons why international financial institutions were able to issue international bonds denominated in currencies other than the five major currencies.

6 Specifically, La Porta et al. (1998) classify countries into those with civil and common law origin. They find that common law origin countries are characterised by higher efficiency in contract enforcement. Common law countries are also documented to offer stronger legal protection of outside investors' rights, for both shareholders and creditors. The legal decision process is also more predictable in common law systems. From these observations, La Porta et al. assert that common law systems are inherently superior to civil code legal systems in encouraging financial and economic development. By contrast, Ahn and Chan-Lee (2001) suggest that better enforcement rather than legal origins are critical.

7 The number is based on the domestic ratings of AA- or higher. If criterion is lowered to A+, the number increases to 49.

Appendix 2.1
The Samurai bondmarket

Samurai bonds are yen-denominated bonds issued in Japan by non-resident issuers. Samurai is a primary offering in Japan under Japanese law.

From the viewpoint of investors, Samurai bonds are considered to be domestic bonds, ensuring easier access than the Eurobond (Japanese institutional investors have stricter investment policies imposed on them when investing in overseas-issued bonds). In addition, the convenience of bond settlement (they can settle Samurai bond based on TKY time), and documentation in Japanese, also provide access to Samurai bonds.

In its 30-year history, the Samurai market gradually evolved and the amount of issuance surged at 3.87 trillion yen in 1996 after the Japanese government lifted the regulation, which prohibited the issuance of sub-investment grade issuers in December 1995. The market experienced a practical closure in 1998 following the East Asian crisis. Since 1999, investors have come back gradually, and the issue amount recovered to 2.3 trillion yen in 2000 then again reduced its size in 2001 at 1.5 trillion yen, affected by the series of credit events.

In 2002, 4 issuers (7 issues) have tapped the Samurai market. Followed by the demand from Japanese investors for high-rated issues, a series of famous global name came to the market. For example, General Electric Capital Corp. (AAA/Aaa), the financing unit of General Electric Co., became the second largest Samurai to date after DaimlerChrysler's 220 billion yen deal launched in November 2000. At first, they planned to issue the Samurai with the amount of 160 billion yen, but backed by the strong demand from investors, GECC increased the total amount to 200 billion yen.

Appendix 2.2
The Singapore Corporate Bondmarket

The development of debt markets in Singapore has been one of the key components of the Monetary Authority of Singapore's attempt to enhance Singapore's role as an international financial centre. This has led to a series of bold reforms, including the liberalisation of the Singapore dollar and the development of Singapore as a hub for issuing, arranging and trading debt securities. The debt markets in Singapore are made up of three major segments: the Singapore government securities market, the Asian dollar bondmarket and the Singapore dollar corporate bondmarket. Despite the fact that the government has run budget surpluses since the 1980s and maintains huge reserves, the Singapore government securities market remains the biggest segment of the debt markets in Singapore. The Asian dollar bondmarket, which involves bonds denominated in non-Singapore dollars, is the second largest even though it has been promoted by the Monetary Authority of Singapore since 1971 to transform Singapore as a financial centre. While remaining as the smallest segment, the Singapore dollar corporate bondmarket has experienced phenomenal growth since 1989 when the Monetary Authority of Singapore began to promote it actively.

Although these markets form the three important pillars of the debt markets in Singapore, the Monetary Authority of Singapore has, in recent years, been focusing on developing the Singapore government securities and Singapore dollar corporate bondmarkets. One reason for this new focus is that the incentives given to the Asian dollar bondmarket are already attractive. The Asian dollar bond has all along been exempted from withholding tax, and banks have been enjoying a concessionary tax rate of 10 per cent on income derived from arranging such bonds. The second reason is that the Singapore government securities and Singapore dollar corporate bondmarkets are of great strategic importance to Singapore, as their absence (or underdevelopment) may imply that Singapore has the problem known as 'original sin'. According to Eichengreen and Hausmann (1999), a country suffers from 'original sin' if it cannot borrow domestic currency in international markets. The East Asian financial crisis has shown vividly that financial fragility is inevitable if domestic investments are financed by foreign currency loans (currency mismatch) or by short-term loans (maturity mismatch). Hence, it is imperative for countries to avoid the 'original sin'.

Growth and structure of the debt markets in Singapore

Singapore government securities, Asian dollar bonds and Singapore dollar corporate bondmarkets have all exhibited strong growth in recent years. The Singapore government securities market still dominates the debt markets in Singapore, with the total gross issuance in 2001 amounting to some S$58.6 billion (S$44.4 billion for treasury bills and S$14.2 billion for bonds). This brought the total Singapore government securities outstanding at end-2001 to S$58.6 billion. The Asian dollar bondmarket is the second largest segment of the debt markets in Singapore. Since its inception in 1971, the Asian dollar bondmarket has grown rapidly, although the level of activity fluctuates from year to year in response to demand for funds by foreign issuers. In 2001, total issuance of the Asian dollar bond was S$50 billion, an increase of 39 per cent over 2000. The fledgling Singapore dollar corporate bondmarket remains the smallest although it has shown rapid growth in recent years. In 2001, total issuance of the Singapore dollar corporate bond was S$22.01 billion, which represents 38 per cent of the total Singapore government securities issuance.

This was a vast improvement over the situation in 2000 when the total issuance of the Singapore dollar corporate bond was only 26 per cent of the total Singapore government securities issuance.

Structure of the Singapore government securities market

The Monetary Authority of Singapore, acting as fiscal agent for the government, issues three-month treasury bills weekly, while one-year treasury bills, as well as two, five, seven and 10 year bonds are issued regularly. In an effort to boost liquidity in the Singapore government securities market, the Monetary Authority of Singapore has announced in May 2000 that all benchmark issues will be at least S$2–2.5 billion in size (Monetary Authority of Singapore 2001a:54). In the 5-year bond auction in 2001, a new benchmark size of S$3.4 billion was established in response to market demand.

The Singapore government securities auctions are held under a Dutch auction process, although bidders at bond auctions may also tender non-competitive bids. All bids must be placed through the eleven primary dealers. In order to ensure that the Singapore government securities auctions are fully taken up, each primary dealer is required to subscribe 1/n of the auction amount, where n is the number of primary dealers. The primary dealers must also provide liquidity to the Singapore government securities and the Singapore government securities repurchase market by quoting continuous two-way prices in Singapore government securities under any trading condition.

The secondary market comprises 38 dealers spread across banks, merchant banks and stockbroking firms. These dealers can trade with retail customers in principal amounts ranging from S$1,000 for Singapore government securities to S$250,000 for Singapore dollar corporate bonds. They trade with each other in standard lot sizes of S$5 million for on-the-run issues, and S$2 million for off-the-run issues. Trading is usually transacted by telephone and cleared electronically on a delivery versus payment basis over the the Monetary Authority of Singapore Electronic Payment System and the Singapore government securities Book-Entry Clearing System operated by the Monetary Authority of Singapore. Introduced in July 1998, this is the real time gross settlement system that replaces the former end-day net settlement system.

The repurchase market has become increasingly liberalised, as the Monetary Authority of Singapore recognises that active development of this market would enable investors and primary dealers to finance their bond inventories and hedge their Singapore dollar debt positions. This would, in turn, facilitate more active trading of Singapore government securities and improve the liquidity in the cash bondmarket. In May 2000, offshore banks were allowed to engage in repurchase without size restriction, lifting the limit of S$20 million set in November 1999. In November 2000, the Monetary Authority of Singapore took the unprecedented step of carrying out its own Singapore government securities repurchase program, aimed at re-channelling liquidity from off-the-run issues into larger and more liquid benchmark bonds. In December 2000, the Monetary Authority of Singapore allowed non-residents to borrow Singapore dollars in the repurchase market without size restriction, provided that the funds are to be used for investment in onshore assets. As a result, the repurchase turnover has grown rapidly since the middle of 1990s. By 2001, the average daily repurchase volume reached S$1.8 billion, about the equivalent of the previous five years' average daily repurchase volume combined (see Appendix Figure 2.1).

The growth of the repurchase transaction has, in turn, facilitated a more active trading of the Singapore government securities and improved liquidity in the cash bondmarket. Turnover of Singapore government securities has been trending upwards in recent years, except for 1999 which saw the defensive behaviour on the part of market participants prior to the run-up to Y2K.

The major holders of the Singapore government securities are banks and finance companies. Banks hold Singapore government securities to meet their minimum liquid asset requirement that currently stands at 18 per cent of their total liability base. Of this 18 per cent, 10 percentage points must be in outright

Appendix Figure 2.1 **Repurchase daily average turnover, 1998–2001 (S$ million)**

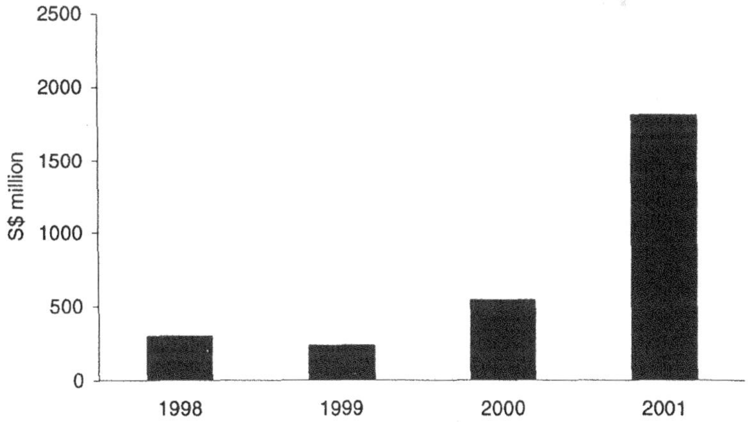

Source: Monetary Authority of Singapore.

Appendix Table 2.1 **Difference between Samurai bonds and Eurobonds**

	Samurai	Eurobond *Uridashi*
Governing law of agreements	Japanese law	Issuer's choice
Related Japanese law	Securities and Exchange law Foreign Exchange and Foreign Trade law	Securities and Exchange law Foreign Exchange and Foreign Trade law in the case of 'Euroyen'
Category	Japanese domestic bond	International bond
Parties concerned	Managers/underwriters/commissioned companies/recording agency/paying agents/Japanese lawyers and CPA	Dealer/seller in Japan/fiscal agent/ trustee/calculation agent/ Japanese lawyer and CPA
Distribution in Japan	Institutional and retail: 100% in Japan	Institutional and retail: mainly retail targeted distribution
Form of the bond	Bearer, definitive/recorded form	Bearer, global form
Clearing and settlement	Physical delivery/recording book	Euroclear/Cedel
Payment system	Japanese paying agents	Fiscal agent/Japanese securities houses
Signing	Tokyo	London
Syndicate group	Mainly Japanese securities houses	Usually no syndicate group, selling group in Japan may be formed

Note: A secondary public offering of existing securities is called *Uridashi* in Japanese. *Uridashi* is defined as a 'secondary public offering' of securities that are once issued in a market outside of Japan (Euromarket) and brought into the Japanese market as existing securities for a public offering. For example, the bonds are underwritten by Nomura International plc in the Euromarket and then marketed to retail investors in Japan through a secondary public offering by The Nomura Securities Co., Ltd.

Appendix Table 2.2 **International corporations' issues, Samurai market 2002**

Issuer	Region	Issuer category	Rating	Type date	Launch date	Maturity (¥ bn)	Amount (years)	Maturity (%)	Coupon price	Issue	Book runner	Target	Spread (bps)
IBM	US	Corp	A1/A+	Str[b]	21/2/2002	4/3/2004	26.00	3	0.6	100.000	Nomura	I[d]	L+29
IBRD	Supra	Supra	AAA	RD[c]	26/2/2002	12/3/2032	10.00	30	Var5.0	100.000	Daiwa SB	I	
IBRD	Supra	Supra	AAA	RD	27/2/2002	12/3/2032	10.00	30	Var5.0	100.000	Mizuho Sec	I	
BMW Finance	EUR	Corp	AA(R&I)	Str	3/6/2002	14/6/2007	45.00	5	0.73	100.000	Daiwa SB	R[e]	L+20
GECC	US	Corp	Aaa/AAA	Str	5/6/2002	17/12/2003	65.00	1.5	3MYL +10bp	100.000	MSDW	I	
GECC	US	Corp	Aaa/AAA	Str	5/6/2002	17/6/2005	65.00	3	0.4	99.970	MSDW	I	L+15
GECC	US	Corp	Aaa/AAA	Str	5/6/2002	17/6/2007	50.00	5	0.73	100.000	MSDW	I	L+20
GECC	US	Corp	Aaa/AAA	Str	5/6/2002	17/6/2012	20.00	10	1.63	99.950	MSDW	I	L+27
Croatia	EUR	Sovereign	BBB-/ BBB(R&I)	Str	12/6/2002	26/6/2008	25.00	6	2.15	100.000	Nomura	R/I	L+144
IBFD	Supra	Supra	AAA	RD	19/6/2002	24/3/2023	3.00	20.75	Var3.0	100.000	Daiwa SB	I	
IBFD	Supra	Supra	AAA	RD	20/6/2002	25/3/2032	1.10	29.75	Var3.5	100.000	Daiwa SB	I	
AFLAC	US	Corp	A/A2/A+(FI)	Str	27/6/2002	27/6/2007	30.00	5	0.96	100.000	Goldman Sachs	I	L+48
KDB[a]	Asia	Sovereign	A3/BBB+ /A-(R&I)	Str	3/7/2002	25/7/2007	30.00	5	0.91	100.000	Daiwa SB	I	L+41

[a] Korea Development Bank
[b] Straight bond, [c] Reverse dual
[d] Institutional investors
[e] Retail investors

Appendix Table 2.3 **Samurai bonds by credit rating, 1990–2002** (billion yen)

Year	AAA	AA	A	BBB	BB	B
1990	181.0	194.0	175.0			
1991	30.0	105.0	255.0	70.0		
1992	214.0	295.0	390.0	280.0		
1993	270.0	331.0	594.0	485.0		
1994	25.0	175.0	393.5	474.0		
1995		312.5	267.0	427.0		
1996		143.0	217.2	379.0	532.0	
1997		79.3	260.5	147.5	150.0	30.0
1998				30.0	32.5	
1999	160.0	150.0	130.0	156.0	50.0	
2000		395.0	1,030.0	187.0	466.5	40.0
2001		205.0	425.0	333.0	400.0	
2002	200.0	45.0	111.0	25.0		

Source: Monetary Authority of Singapore.

Appendix Table 2.4 **Samurai bonds by tenors, 1990–2002**

Year	1–3 yrs	4–5 yrs	6–7 yrs	8–10 yrs	11–20 yrs	20 yrs
1990	10.0	192.0	170.0	178.0		
1991		75.0	170.0	215.0		
1992	60.0	430.0	315.0	374.0		
1993	30.0	741.5	304.0	474.5	60.0	70.0
1994	207.0	491.0	180.0	170.0	20.0	
1995	35.0	401.0	222.0	159.0	140.0	50.0
1996	52.0	491.5	330.0	244.0	65.0	88.7
1997	56.0	174.5	210.0	98.3	116.0	12.5
1998	22.5	30.0				
1999	410.0	159.0	30.0	47.0		
2000	790.0	1,118.5	85.0	125.0		
2001	494.0	693.0	163.0	13.0		
2002	166.0	170.0	25.0	20.0		

Source: Monetary Authority of Singapore.

holdings of Singapore government securities while up to 4 percentage points may be in the form of trade bills. From May 2000 onwards, term reverse repurchase transactions (or loans taken by banks using Singapore government securities as collateral) are eligible for up to 5 percentage points of the minimum liquid asset requirement (Monetary Authority of Singapore 2001a:37). In the past, only overnight repurchase trades are eligible for the minimum liquid asset requirement. At the end of 2000, the total minimum liquid asset requirement was S$35.3 billion, compared with S$43.2 billion of Singapore government securities outstanding. But the actual liquid assets held by banks in 2000 was S$39.5 billion, which was some S$4.2 billion in excess of the minimum liquid asset requirement. Out of these S$39.5 billion of liquid assets held by banks, some S$33.7 billion (or 78 per cent) were Singapore government securities. It can thus be seen that a large chunk of the Singapore government securities is being 'locked up' by banks.

It is frequently stated that the government-run pension fund, the Central Provident Fund, is the single largest holder of government bonds. However, the bonds that it holds are of a particular kind. These are specially-issued, non-tradable, long-term government bonds which are held by the Central Provident Fund until maturity. In 2000, the Fund held some S$60.6 billion of such bonds, which was one and a half times more than the total Singapore government securities outstanding (Monetary Authority of Singapore 2001a:107). Most of the proceeds from such bonds are probably channelled to the Government of Singapore Investment Corporation for investment in foreign assets.

Structure of the Asian dollar bondmarket

The first Asian dollar bond was launched by the Development Bank of Singapore in December 1971 when it floated a US$10 million 10-year issue. Since then, many other banks and corporations (both domestic and international) as well as national governments and multilateral organisations have tapped this source of funds. The type of issuers varies from year to year. Most of the Asian dollar bond issues were denominated in US dollars. 2001 was a typical year when some 92 per cent of the Asian dollar bondmarket were denominated in US dollars, with the remaining 8 per cent denominated in Hong Kong dollar, euro and Japanese yen (Monetary Authority of Singapore 2001b:7).

Structure of the Singapore dollar corporate bondmarket

The Singapore dollar corporate bondmarket has been markedly transformed in recent years. In 1998, property companies were the dominant issuers, accounting for about 70 per cent of total issuance in the Singapore dollar

Appendix Figure 2.2 **Profile of Singapore dollar debt issuers**

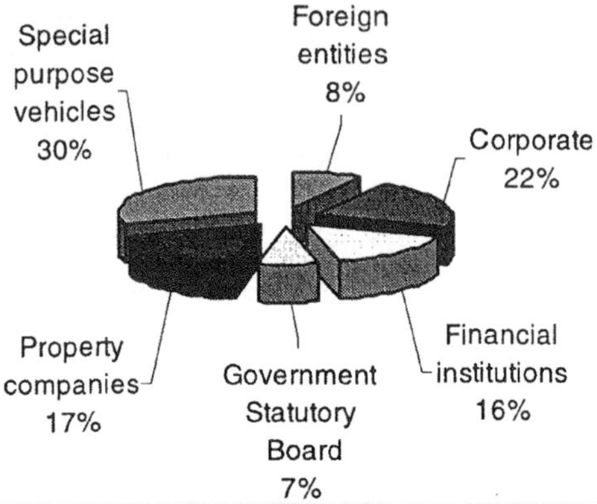

Source: Monetary Authority of Singapore, 2003. *Survey of the Singapore Corporate Debt Market*, Monetary Authority of Singapore, Singapore. Available online at http://www.mas.gov.sg/singfinsec/download/2002DebtSurvey.pdf.

corporate bondmarket. By 2001, the issuer mix has become more balanced, with property companies accounting for only 17 per cent of the debt issuance. Other major issuers in 2001 were financial institutions (16 per cent), statutory boards (7 per cent) and foreign entities (8 per cent). 2001 was an unusual year for financial institutions as they were exceptionally active in the Singapore dollar corporate bondmarket to raise funds for their merger and acquisition activities (see Appendix Figure 2.2). The rising importance of statutory boards and foreign entities in the Singapore debt market scene did not occur by accident. Rather, it is the result of a deliberate two-pronged strategy by the Monetary Authority of Singapore to promote the corporate bondmarket.

The first prong in the development plan has been the encouragement given to statutory boards and government-linked corporations to tap the bondmarkets rather than opt for direct bank lending. Learning from the experience of the crisis-hit economies in East Asia, where their balance sheets were under extreme stress because of the concentration on bank lending, the Monetary Authority of Singapore was keen to diversify these risks. The development of the corporate bondmarket therefore allows companies to diversify funding sources and reduce their dependence on bank lending. Apart from increasing the size of the corporate bondmarket, the issues by statutory boards have extended the yield curve, with the Jurong Town Corporation launching a S$200 million 12-year issue in 2000. Singapore Telecommunications, a government-linked corporation, also responded to the call by the government by launching a S$1 billion 5-year issue in February 2001, the largest issuance in the Singapore dollar corporate bondmarket to date. In addition to straight fixed and floating rate straight debt, local corporations also issued mortgaged-backed securities and other innovative synthetic mortgaged-backed securities.

The second prong of the approach has been the opening up of the Singapore dollar bondmarket to foreign issuers. This is accomplished through the Monetary Authority of Singapore's Notice 757, introduced in August 1998 and amended in November 1999. The main points of these notices are as follows.

- If the Singapore dollar proceeds from bond issuance are to be used outside Singapore, they must be converted or swapped into foreign currency before remitting abroad.
- The swap leg of the above transaction is exempted from the cash and minimum liquid asset requirements and from tax.
- There is no minimum size requirement (the minimum issue size was S$100 million when Notice 757 was first issued).
- There is no restriction on the credit rating of issuers.
- If funds raised are for use in Singapore, issues for non-bank non-residents do not require prior approval from the Monetary Authority of Singapore.

Despite the condition requiring foreign issuers to convert or swap their Singapore dollar proceeds into a foreign currency before remitting abroad, many of them have come to the Singapore dollar corporate bondmarket. This basic requirement has not hindered legitimate foreign issuers from tapping the Singapore market. Indeed, from the introduction of the Notice 757 in August 1998 up till the first quarter of 2002, some S$7.2 billion of Singapore

Appendix Table 2.5 **Size of the capital market, 2001** (US$ billion)

	Stock market capitalisation	%	Debt securities	%	Bank assets	%
World	28,875.1	19.2	41,792.2	27.8	79,401.8	52.9
EU-15	6,763.0	13.1	11,843.4	23	32,939.7	63.9
United States	13,826.6	25.4	18,504.3	34	22,157.4	40.7
Japan	2,293.8	10.6	6,925.1	32	12,408.6	57.4
Asia	1,310.4	14.1	1,270.0	13.7	6,722.4	72.3
Latin America	412.0	15.3	693.7	25.7	1,593.3	59

Source: International Monetary Fund, 2003. *Global Financial Stability Report: market developments and issues*, International Monetary Fund, Washington, DC. Available online at http://www.imf.org/External/Pubs/FT/GFSR/2003/01/index.htm.

Appendix Table 2.6 **Sources of corporate finance, 2000** (US$ billion)

	Bank loans	Corporate bonds	Equities
Korea	59.6	25.9	36.4
Indonesia	60.2	1.7	20.1
Malaysia	122.7	9.2	83.6
Thailand	99.2	4.2	26.3
United States	38.9	45.4	178.9

Source: International Monetary Fund, 2003. *Global Financial Stability Report: market developments and issues*, March, International Monetary Fund, Washington, DC. Available online at http://www.imf.org/External/Pubs/FT/GFSR/2003/01/index.htm.

dollar debts have been issued by foreign entities. The issue size ranged from S$25 million to S$400 million. Tenures of bonds were generally extended, in some cases to as long as 10 years.

Many supra-nationals and multinationals have been quick to make their debut in Singapore in order to raise the visibility of their organisations. Foreign issuers might also be attracted to the Singapore market because of the low borrowing cost and large pool of Singapore dollar funds. However, combining a Singapore dollar loan with a currency swap would result in a 'synthetic' foreign currency loan for foreign issuers. Given that the swap market involving the Singapore dollar is illiquid and has wide spreads, it is unclear whether foreign issuers would still come to Singapore when they could issue foreign currency bonds directly in the Eurodollar bondmarket. If not, many potential foreign issuers might just wait until Singapore is able to develop a more liquid swap market.

Rationale for developing the Singapore government securities and the Singapore dollar corporate bondmarkets

The over-dependence on bank lending and short-term capital inflows to finance long-term investments has often been cited as one of the main reasons for the East Asian financial crisis in 1997. It had been argued that the crisis might have been avoided if a well-developed bondmarket had existed in the region, as Asian governments and companies would then have a more stable source of long-term domestic currency funding rather than short-term foreign loans. However, the rationale for developing the debt market in the East Asian region after the crisis does not seem to be particularly relevant to Singapore for various reasons. First, the government and many of the large companies in

Singapore do not need to borrow, as they are generally cash-rich. Second, Singapore's sophisticated bank lending network and equity capital market will probably more than compensate for the absence of bondmarkets and continue to be the fundraising avenues of choice. Third, the banking sector is so well capitalised and well regulated that banks' over-exposure in foreign currencies is unlikely to happen in Singapore. Hence, the need to develop the debt markets in Singapore is probably governed by other imperatives.

One imperative is the desire on the part of the government to develop the island state as a financial services hub for the region. Currently, Singapore is laying a strong foundation for developing the regional bondmarket. For a start, Singapore is encouraging well-established foreign entities to issue and purchase Singapore dollar bonds, in its effort to emulate Switzerland where foreigners are active issuers and traders of Swiss franc bonds. In the longer term, Singapore is aspiring to become the centre for the issuing and trading of regional currency bonds.

The second motivation for developing the Singapore bondmarket is that the growth of liabilities in the banking, insurance and asset management industries creates a need for a larger asset base. While issuance of Singapore government securities is constrained by fiscal surpluses, issuance by local corporations is limited by their investment opportunities. For this reason, encouraging the issuance of Singapore dollar bonds by foreign entities is a necessary step to meet the asset needs of Singapore's various financial institutions.

It can be surmised that the development of the Singapore government securities market has had a positive effect on the development of the Singapore dollar corporate bondmarket. First, the securities market has provided the necessary benchmark yield curve for the pricing of the Singapore dollar corporate bond. Second, it helps to educate the investing public about the intricacies of bond investment. Third, the active participation of residents in the Singapore government securities market can only enhance the ability of Singapore firms to borrow in Singapore dollars. The reasoning is that if government bonds are widely held by domestic investors, there will be a strong political constituency against any surprise inflation engineered by the government (Eichengreen and Hausmann 1999). As a result, non-residents will be more willing to hold bonds denominated in the domestic currency. The only negative effect from the development of the Singapore government securities market is the possible 'crowding out' of the Singapore dollar corporate bondmarket. Thus far, the growth of the Singapore government securities market does not seem to be crowding out the Singapore dollar corporate bondmarket.

Factors hindering bondmarket development in Singapore

The main factors hindering the development of Singapore's debt markets are constraints in supply and demand.

On the supply side, the small domestic market of Singapore severely limits the amount of funds that its government and local corporations would need. In addition, it is relative easy for statutory boards and corporations in Singapore to obtain bank credit; issuing bonds is apparently more troublesome and time consuming. The fact that the debt markets in Singapore are largely a captive market has exacerbated the problem. For example, a high proportion of Singapore government securities are held by commercial banks and finance companies to fulfil the minimum liquid asset requirement. Singapore government securities are also held—usually to maturity—by insurance companies. As a result of this captive market, there is little trading of these securities in the secondary market.

On the demand side, most of the Singapore investors have strong preference for equities and properties over bonds. Because of the low interest rate environment in Singapore, the yields on bonds, particularly government bonds, are low and unattractive. On top of that, Singapore investors have to pay tax on interest income whereas they do not have to pay tax on capital gains obtained from investing in equities and properties. Last, but not least, bond trading in the over-the-counter market lacks liquidity and transparency. As a result, bond investors tend to buy and hold their bonds rather than trade actively.

Most of the investors of Singapore dollar corporate bonds are insurance companies and fund managers operating in Singapore. Hence, the Singapore dollar corporate bondmarket has a great potential for growth if Singapore is able to tap the local retail market and the international market. There are three possible reasons for the lack of interest on the part of foreign investors. First, the yields on Singapore dollar bonds are relatively low. Second, since the East Asian financial crisis that started in July 1997, the Singapore dollar has depreciated against the US dollar and against a basket of currencies. The depreciating Singapore dollar in the past few years might have reduced the attractiveness of holding Singapore dollar bonds. Third, the illiquid secondary market must have further reduced the incentive of non-residents to hold Singapore dollar bonds as an investment instrument.

3 Promoting Asian basket currency bonds

Takatoshi Ito

With many Asian countries experiencing robust growth since 1999, the East Asian currency crisis of 1997–98 seems to be just a distant memory. However, just when you think you are in safe waters, perils may sneak up on you again. Some countries, such as Thailand and Indonesia, are experiencing strong capital inflows and the currencies may be appreciating beyond levels that might be justified by the fundamentals.

Many of the recommendations that were identified after the crisis have not been implemented. Three of these recommendations are examined in this chapter.

- Reduce vulnerability to avoid the double mismatch problem, namely currency and maturity mismatches of borrowers in emerging market companies—to borrow short in US dollars and lend long in local currency is dangerous.
- Avoid over-reliance on the banking sector, since a twin crisis (a simultaneous currency and banking crisis) is damaging to the economy.
- Avoid the dollar peg, both from the viewpoint of maintaining price competitiveness of imports and of discouraging too many short-term capital inflows.

Reliance on the banking system can be reduced by promotion of bond financing. If the government and corporations can issue bonds for long-term projects then they can reduce borrowing from banks. Banks also benefit from avoiding maturity mismatch. One of the problems is that bondmarkets in emerging market economies have not been developed in terms of market institutions. The bondmarket in an emerging market may benefit from an effort to broaden the market to the region, since inviting foreign investors will deepen the market. However, in order to attract investors into the bondmarket, transparency may have to be enhanced. Therefore, it is desirable to establish a region-wide bondmarket.

Asian bonds have been proposed, most prominently by Prime Minister Thaksin of Thailand. The Asian bond has become a focal point for regional financial cooperation after the Chiang Mai Initiative.

Asian bonds

Asian bonds are issued by Asian institutions (governments, corporations, and financial institutions), denominated in an Asian currency, rated by Asian rating agencies, and sold, traded, cleared and settled at an Asian financial centre (Tokyo, Singapore or Hong Kong SAR). Investors are expected to be mainly regional (Japan, Singapore and Hong Kong SAR in particular), but other investors are welcome. The components of an Asian bond are the issuer, the currency denomination and the location of a secondary market. Even if only two of the three conditions are met, they may still be called Asian bonds. Rating agencies would assist in creating a market, and Asian investors are naturally more attracted to Asian bonds than are outside investors.

In order to solve the double mismatch problem (discussed in earlier chapters), it is essential that Asian bonds be issued in a local currency, or a basket of local currencies. By issuing bonds in the local currency, governments or corporations are freed from the possibility of an acute dollar liquidity shortage, unless maturities are bunched in particular months. Major trading centres should be regional so that settlement and clearance transactions can be completed in real time. This can be achieved if regional central banks extend the real time gross settlement facility to financial centres, and settlement and clearance facilities are developed in regional financial centres.

Investors are known to have a 'home bias', that is, the investor's portfolio—especially in the case of equities—is heavily biased toward domestic securities. Home bias may exist for a number of reasons, including avoidance of currency risk, familiarity with local products and the existence of multinationals. Since home bias exists, there may also be 'regional bias', in that investors may be attracted toward securities issued by countries in the region, second to domestic securities. The currencies in the region are more highly correlated than other currencies, and familiarity with regional companies and currencies is high, that is why major investors into Asian bonds are Asian investors.

Objectives of promoting Asian bonds

Asian bonds provide financial instruments to avoid double mismatch. Second, they develop a market and a channel of converting regional saving to regional investment, creating a bridge between investors and corporate/government borrowers. As the region is expected to maintain high economic growth, good investment opportunities exist. The region is also known to be populated with strong savers. Third, spreading risk from the banking sector to other financial institutions will lessen the risk of another severe financial crisis; this strategy avoids a twin crisis.

Let us examine two questions. Who would be the issuers and the borrowers if a well-functioning bondmarket was established and what would be the benefits for them? Borrowers will benefit from issuing bonds in local currencies and can match revenues in local currencies by borrowing in local currencies. Corporations exporting within the region also can issue liabilities in the destination currencies of their exports.

By issuing bonds instead of borrowing from banks, corporations can diversify risk. Even when banks fall into financial difficulties, corporations have alternative funding sources. Risk will be diversified. Better-funded corporations can borrow, even at low rates. Capital costs will be thus lowered.

Investors in the region can also benefit from having alternative investment opportunities. They would welcome high quality Asian-currency denominated bonds and would offer a reasonable risk-yield trade-off.

One of the puzzles in financial economics is home bias—investors hold domestic securities (equities and bonds) in a far higher proportion than theoretically warranted. Home bias can be rooted in familiarity and aversion to currency risk. If these are the reasons for home bias, there could be 'regional bias'. Japanese investors could may find Korean and Thailand firms more familiar than Latin American and Central European firms.

After the East Asian currency crisis, most Asian currencies are floating. The correlation of an Asian currency with the yen has increased after the crisis, although the correlation coefficient seems to fluctuate, the currency risk of Asian bonds (denominated in Asian currencies) for Asian investors must be less than that of bonds denominated in US dollars or the euro.

Despite the benefits of the Asian bondmarket, there are obstacles to quick establishment. Disclosure and transparency of Asian securities and borrowers are not as good as the United States and European counterparts. The legal and market infrastructure of the bondmarket is also weak.

The Asian Bond Fund

In June 2003, the Executives' Meeting of East Asia-Pacific Central Banks (whose members consist of central banks of Australia, China, Hong Kong SAR, Indonesia, Japan, Korea, Malaysia, New Zealand, the Philippines, Singapore and Thailand) announced that they would contribute US$1 billion to the Asian Bond Fund, managed by the Bank for International Settlements, in order to invest in dollar-denominated, sovereign and quasi-sovereign bonds issued by Asian issuers.[1] The central banks will set aside a portion of their foreign reserves (estimated to be more than US$1 trillion) to invest in the Fund. Eligible securities are those issued by governments and quasi-governments.

Will the Asian Bond Fund help the creation of the Asian bondmarket? The Asian Bond Fund is, at best, a good step toward an eventual development of the Asian bondmarket. However, this proposal does not exactly fit what was envisioned as Asian bonds. First, the use of the US dollar, presumed in the current version of the Asian Bond Fund, does not contribute to the financial and monetary stability of the region. Thus establishing and enlarging the Asian Bond Fund will not avoid the double mismatch problem. Second, under the current version of the Asian Bond Fund, monetary authorities buy and hold Asian bonds as foreign exchange, so a secondary market of Asian bonds will not develop. Third, central banks contributed to the Asian Bond Fund, but foreign reserves are strictly regulated as eligible securities. That is why investment is limited to sovereign and quasi-sovereign bonds. Due to the regulation, the market size of bonds in which the Asian Bond Fund can invest will be limited. However, promoting corporate bonds and asset-backed securities is very important for the region.

A new direction is needed. One idea is to broaden the asset class of the Asian Bond Fund. Suppose that the central banks decide to establish Asian Bond Fund II, able to invest in local-currency denominated bonds. This solves the first problem—helping countries to avoid the double mismatch problem. Even if this happens, the (quasi) sovereign bond condition is difficult to remove, so long as the central banks desire the funds to be counted toward foreign reserves. Lower credit-rated securities, such as corporate bonds or asset-backed securities would not qualify for foreign reserves.

Another idea is to promote issues, trade and investment in Asian bonds by private sector participants. Government bonds denominated in local currency should be issued in order to provide a benchmark for private issues. A main objective would be to nurture corporate bonds and asset-backed securities issues in local currency, being traded regionally.

Current role of bonds in Asia

Let us review how bonds are issued and traded in Asia today (see also Rhee 2003). Table 3.1 shows the size of bank loans, stockmarket capitalisation, government bonds and corporate bonds of Asian countries, with Japan and United States as reference, for 1997 and 2002. In all countries, except the Philippines and Indonesia (in 2002), bank loans are much bigger than government bonds. Since many Asian countries adopted a balanced budget policy, government bond issues before the currency crisis were very limited. Only after the currency crisis did government bond issues increase sharply to finance budget deficits. Government bonds in Indonesia increased sharply due to recapitalisation of banks by government bonds. After the currency crisis of 1997–98, banks in Indonesia suffered massive losses and most banks became insolvent. The government injected large amounts of capital into many banks in the form of government bonds. In 2002, about 90 per cent of government bonds were held by commercial banks for the purpose of recapitalisation. These bonds could be sold for cash, and there is a tendency for bonds to have been made into mutual funds and sold to investors. This may help to establish the government bondmarket.

Many Asian countries increased the amount of government bond issues after the currency crisis of 1997–98. For example, Indonesia had not used government bonds before the crisis, as its regular budget was balanced, although its development budget was financed by borrowing from abroad. However, bond issues increased sharply after the crisis, especially because of the need to finance deficits caused by bank recapitalisation. Bonds were issued specifically for that purpose, thus they were called recapitalisation bonds. Some of the recapitalisation bonds are not allowed to be sold, but others can be sold to investors. In 2002 and 2003, some of recapitalisation bonds were sold to mutual funds. The frequency and total size of the secondary market transactions are still very low (Table 3.2 and Table 3.3).

The size of corporate bonds is very small in all countries except Singapore, where the size is comparable to the United States. In the United States, corporate bonds are bigger than bank loans, stockmarket and capitalisation exceeds GDP in Malaysia, Singapore and Hong Kong SAR. The capitalisation ratio of these three economies exceeds that of the United States. The ratio of government bonds to GDP increased in all East Asian countries from 1997 to 2002, while the ratio declined in the United States. The ratio of corporate bonds to GDP also increased in all East Asian countries, except in Indonesia.

There was a sharp increase in government bond issues from 1997 to 1999 in several countries, including Indonesia, Thailand and Korea in the wake of

Table 3.1 **Size of capital markets of East Asian countries and the United States, 1997 and 2002** (US$ billion)

	Outstanding balance of bank loans		Total market capitalisation		Outstanding balance of government bonds		Outstanding balance of corporate bonds	
	1997	2002	1997	2002	1997	2002	1997	2002
Indonesia	60	23	25	17	-	40	3	1
Malaysia	98	94	133	133	24	30	17	29
Philippines	60	37	52	52	61	79	5	..
Thailand	121	81	23	37	5	21	3	5
Korea	44	79	16	43	6	17	20	30
Taiwan	112	119	116	93	12	23	4	14
Singapore	101	103	233	185	16	37	22	57
Hong Kong SAR	152	144	238	284	8	9	19	33
China	106	169	24	37	7	19	1	1
Japan	101	85	54	50	49	99	7	12
United States	37	40	159	112	45	35	43	59

Source: Yamagami, H., 2003. 'Asian bond market —a scheme for ABS issuers', Japanese Bankers Association, *Kin-yu*, November:2–15.

Table 3.2 **Government bonds ownership in Indonesia, 2000–2002** (million rupiah)

	2000	2001	2002	Per cent
Ministry of Finance	-	877,545	872,545	0.2
Recap banks	390,143,372	356,271,301	334,573,956	79.8
State banks	250,184,352	235,422,965	228,176,234	54.5
Private banks	32,649,312	29,772,917	22,646,557	5.4
Taken-over banks	106,079,258	89,844,969	82,538,678	19.7
Regional development banks	1,230,450	1,230,450	1,212,487	0.3
Non-recap banks	6,954,361	24,772,569	13,829,234	3.3
Sub-registry	1,823,861	13,022,018	44,782,147	10.7
Insurance	1,042,611	3,758,511	6,512,792	1.6
Mutual fund	16,500	2,025,284	35,719,912	8.5
Pension fund	5,750	160,750,6	360,411	0.1
IBRA	755,000	6,661,328	1,908,124	0.5
Corporate	2,000	109,177	71,880	-
Securities	-	301,968	133,603	-
Foundation	-	3,000	-	-
Individual	-	2,000	-	-
Others	-	-	75,425	-
Hedge bonds (non-tradable)	32,880,567	40,359,512	25,298,505	6.0
Recapitalisation—state banks	32,880,567	28,477,503	18,173,654	4.3
Recapitalisation—private banks	-	11,882,009	7,124,850	1.7
Total	431,802,161	435,302,945	419,356,387	100

Source: Subiyantoro, H., and Ginting, L., S., 2003. Indonesian government bonds market development, Paper presented at Asian Bond Symposium, Keic University, Japan, February.

the currency crisis. Government bonds in Taiwan, Korea, Indonesia and Thailand increased substantially from 2001 to 2002 (Table 3.4).

From 1997 to 2002, there was a trend towards corporate bonds in all countries except Indonesia and the Philippines. Outstanding amounts more than doubled in Malaysia, Taiwan and Singapore (Table 3.5).

Those economies most severely hit by the currency crisis, such as Indonesia, increased their proportion of government bonds but did not increase corporate bonds. Countries that were hit by the currency-banking crisis, such as Thailand, Malaysia, Korea and Singapore, recovered quickly and developed corporate bondmarkets.

In both types of countries bank loans declined, since the currency crisis was accompanied by a banking crisis. A sharp decline shows the danger of over-reliance on bank loans. The impact on the banking sector would have spread to the entire economy quickly, suggesting that the economy would be better off having alternative financing channels, such as corporate bonds.

Table 3.3 **Bond transactions in secondary markets in Indonesia, 2000–2003**

	Corporate bonds		Government bonds	
	Volume (billion rupiah)	Frequency	Volume (billion rupiah)	Frequency
2000	8,791.74	2,495	27,905.83	161
2001	1,048.42	385	66,172.11	1167
2002				
January	144.90	61	6,626.96	214
February	152.00	46	10,562.98	297
March	61.00	22	8,448.65	284
April	630.77	90	3,721.35	187
May	366.12	115	10,460.72	300
June	510.69	204	9,035.66	273
July	633.75	266	14,186.15	396
August	535.00	220	17,302.75	487
September	790.51	311	16,688.59	468
October	1,330.63	409	12,264.51	431
November	381.22	173	10,563.25	439
December	381.22	173	14,186.15	396
2003				
January	416.77	121	17,597.60	581

Source: Subiyantoro, H., and Ginting, L.S., 2003. Indonesian government bonds market development, Paper presented at Asian Bond Symposium, Keio University, Japan, February.

Table 3.4 **Outstanding government bonds, East Asian economies and the United States, 1996–2002**

	1996	1997	1998	1999	2000	2001	2002
Indonesia	..	..	12,461	71,993	68,793	63,468	72,785
Thailand	705	291	11,227	15,676	15,229	15,980	25,836
Malaysia	26,457	17,026	19,740	20,615	23,543	27,224	28,829
Philippines	28,465	18,943	22,008	24,477	21,614	24,723	..
Korea	29,969	16,755	34,551	53,779	56,307	62,703	82,844
Taiwan	36,085	31,742	32,344	39,624	44,708	53,096	63,722
Singapore	14,645	13,065	17,242	21,188	24,973	28,974	33,429
Hong Kong SAR	11,873	13,123	12,581	13,110	13,930	14,589	15,065
China	52,559	66,534	93,803	127,327	157,296	188,696	233,168
Japan	2,109,122	1,985,283	2,554,058	3,245,291	3,198,909	3,309,519	4,142,314
United States	3,755,076	3,778,273	3,723,674	3,652,683	3,357,764	3,352,741	3,609,754

Source: Yamagami, H., 2003. 'Asian bond market —a scheme for ABS issuers', Japanese Bankers Association, *Kin-yu*, November:2–15.

Table 3.5 **Outstanding corporate bonds, East Asian economies and the United States, 1996–2002**

	1996	1997	1998	1999	2000	2001	2002
Indonesia	4,153	3,356	1,807	2,245	2,333	1,994	2,396
Thailand	5,083	2,807	3,430	4,787	4,839	5,692	6,489
Malaysia	13,257	11,972	12,299	20,693	26,446	30,967	27,368
Philippines	22,892	3,006	3,075	..	..	..	..
Korea	90,033	53,160	101,895	105,115	105,692	117,244	151,745
Taiwan	9,110	9,903	19,380	21,913	24,217	28,890	39,839
Singapore	18,574	18,502	19,271	25,810	28,588	43,652	51,368
Hong Kong SAR	25,278	32,668	38,888	43,993	46,626	48,745	53,204
China	7,203	6,293	8,177	9,404	10,409	12,186	..
Japan	265,921	286,876	393,561	488,315	470,138	437,140	499,794
United States	3,205,100	3,594,500	4,187,400	4,626,400	5,022,900	5,692,300	6,207,800

Source: Yamagami, H., 2003. 'Asian bond market —a scheme for ABS issuers', Japanese Bankers Association, *Kin-yu*, November:2–15.

Next, let us consider the question of bonds turnover. Even when outstanding balances of government and corporate bonds increase, the market is not functioning if bonds are held by institutions and not traded. Active trading took place in the secondary market, although most of the trading is over-the-counter rather than at the Korean Stock Exchange (Table 3.6a). Turnover ratios of Indonesia are extremely low, due to the recapitalisation bond phenomenon described above (Table 3.6b). The turnover ratio in Malaysia has been steadily increasing (Table 3.6c).

The data in these tables point to the challenges and potential of the Asian bondmarket. Government bonds may have to be regularly issued, whether funding needs are there or not, so that the market will deepen. The market infrastructure of corporate bonds has to be examined so that alternative funding sources for corporations will be available.

Proposal for an Asian Bond Corporation

In order to achieve the objectives of the Asian Bond Markets Initiative, several steps need to be taken. There are two different kinds of problems: for issuers, any obstacles for potential issuers to issue local-currency denominated bonds should be identified and removed; for investors, if they feel that local-currency denominated bonds issued by Asian issuers are too risky, both in currency and in credit, then those concerns must be examined and allayed. Investors may not correctly interpret information on the quality of issuers if information about the company and credit rating (that is, an aggregate quantification of information) is not readily available and credible to investors. Informational asymmetry would destroy the regional market.

One way to promote Asian bonds is to establish an organisation that can bridge issuers and investors from different economies. Issuers would prefer to issue bonds in local currency, for example the Thai baht, while investors would like to receive returns and principal in their local currency, for example, the yen. Similarly, issuers in different countries would like to issue bonds in local currencies. If the currency risk can be mitigated, investors may be more attracted to the bonds. One way to reduce volatility, or risk, in returns to the yen is to construct a basket of bonds in different currency denominations. Each currency may carry risks, but when they are grouped into a basket, the aggregate risk may be less.

This chapter proposes the establishment of a corporation (an offshore entity) to purchase local currency bonds and transform these into a basket currency bond. The entity may be called the Asian Bond Corporation, and will issue ABC bonds that reflect the value of underlying assets. The basket

Table 3.6a **Korea's bond turnover ratio, 1995–2002**

	1995	1996	1997	1998	1999	2000	2001	2002
Outstanding balance	125,998	175,540	224,117	334,034	364,419	424,684	504,730	563,943
Turnover	231,205	230,363	286,991	856,058	2,400,580	2,237,747	2,938,606	2,210,082
Turnover ratio (times)	1.83	1.31	1.28	2.56	6.59	5.27	5.82	3.92
KSE	1.3	1.2	2.8	3.6	24.5	2.5	0.1	4.2
OTC	98.7	98.8	97.2	96.2	75.5	97.5	99	95.7

Source: Fukuchi, A., 2003. 'Trend of Asian bond market', *Tokyo-Mitsubishi Review*, October:1–8.

Table 3.6b **Malaysia's bond turnover ratio, 1995–2002**

	1995	1996	1997	1998	1999	2000	2001	2002
Outstanding balance	3,846	25,373	12,367	33,085	63,838	88,625	219,942	244,135
Turnover	64,719	66,910	66,262	75,012	78,336	89,050	103,450	109,550
Turnover ratio (times)	0.06	0.38	0.19	0.44	0.81	1.00	2.13	2.23

Source: Fukuchi, A., 2003. 'Trend of Asian bond market', *Tokyo-Mitsubishi Review*, October:1–8.

Table 3.6c **Indonesia's bond turnover ratio, 1998–2002**

	1998	1999	2000	2001	2002
Outstanding balance	100,000	496,600	653,900	695,000	650,700
Turnover				64,546	130,787
Turnover ratio (times)			0.10	0.20	

Source: Fukuchi, A., 2003. 'Trend of Asian bond market', *Tokyo-Mitsubishi Review*, October:1–8.

of bonds by the Asian Bond Corporation would include bonds with the same maturity, so that maturity mismatch would not occur (Chaipravat 2003, Ito 2003a, Oh, Park and Yang 2003).

Since the ABC basket bond is fully backed by the assets of the Asian Bond Corporation, the basket bond has a property of a weighted average of underlying bonds, in terms of currency fluctuation, coupons, and default risk. If the underlying bonds were sovereign, the ABC bond would perform like a sovereign. Credit risk would be minimised unless the issuing government has low credit rating. If the underlying bonds are corporate bonds, basket bonds would carry default risk and premium, similar to the weighted average of risk and premium of the underlying bonds. The ABC sovereign bonds would provide a benchmark for corporate bonds.

Let us consider concrete steps to implement this proposal. The fiscal authorities of Japan, Korea and Thailand, and any other willing Asian countries, should jointly establish the Asian Bond Corporation in offshore market (Tokyo, Hong Kong SAR or Singapore). The Corporation will purchase sovereign bonds (later, corporate bonds and asset-backed securities) of the participating countries, issued in the respective local market and denominated in the yen, won, baht and other currencies. The Asian Bond Corporation's asset side is composed of a basket of bonds in different currency denominations and different coupon rates. The ABC bond, on the liability side of the Asian Bond Corporation, is backed by the market value of the bonds on the asset side. Hence, pricing of ABC bonds in the secondary market should reflect the value of the underlying assets.

For example, we recommend that the Asian Bond Corporation initially purchase Japanese, Korean and Thai government bonds with value-weights of 50–30–20, respectively. Then the pricing of the ABC bond reflects both the exchange rate fluctuations of the yen, the won and the baht, as well as the interest rate movements in the three countries of origin. With respect to currency risk, the ABC bonds show a feature of a basket currency, namely a weighted average of the three currencies. The coupon interest rate of the ABC bond will be a weighted average of the underlying bonds.

Many investors will find ABC bonds attractive. Investors are willing to take some currency and credit risk to receive returns, but risks have to be transparent, fair and diversified. (Japanese investors currently receive only 0.8 per cent yield from holding Japanese bonds, but some of them are eager to purchase Australian dollar-denominated bonds yielding 5 per cent, reflecting currency and credit risk. They may be attracted to an ABC bond yielding 3 per cent, with lower currency risk.) The role of the Asian Bond Corporation is to bundle bonds from diverse sources, so that a reasonable trade-off point in the risk–return curve will be offered in a transparent manner. Regional investors who pursue higher returns without increasing too much of risk will regard bonds issued by the Asian Bond Corporation as just such financial instruments.

If credit risk of participating bonds makes ABC bonds unattractive to risk averse-bond investors in the region, the partial guarantee may be offered by a credit enhancement agency. When corporate bonds and asset-backed securities are bundled into an ABC corporate bond, credit enhancement or separating into senior bonds and junior bonds may help widen the customer base. The role of asset-backed securities is emphasised in Oh et al. (2003), with several novel ways to separate junior and senior bonds. If currency risk, even as a weighted average, is not desirable for some home-biased investors, the Asian Bond Corporation, or its foreign exchange swap partners may offer swap into local currencies. Wong and Ho (this volume) review the role of private credit insurers in the United States.

The ABC sovereign bonds will not assume any major risk, because the value and coupon payments of assets and liability matches all the time. It should behave like a currency board or a mutual fund. The Asian Bond Corporation helps create the Asian bond secondary market. The Corporation encourages the issues of bonds in the region. The ABC sovereign bond should give the benchmark for corporate bonds and Asian Bond Corporation asset-backed securities bonds.

The Asian Bond Corporation proposal has several advantages over the Asian Bond Fund proposal. The Asian Bond Corporation promotes local currency bond issues, while the Asian Bond Fund in the current version invests in the dollar-denominated bonds only. The Asian Bond Corporation will bundle them as a basket-currency bond for investors.

In this proposal, ABC bonds promote the secondary market by issuing bonds, while Asian Bond Fund does not: the central banks in the Asian Bond

Fund are buyer-investor, while the Asian Bond Corporation is an issuer as well as a buyer. ABC bonds will have a secondary market in the country with investors. In this sense, the two proposals are quite complementary, while the Asian Bond Corporation is based on market participants and principles. The Asian Bond Corporation will have no limit on the type of securities in which it may invest, but the Asian Bond Fund will be limited to sovereign and quasi-sovereign bonds. If another crisis occurs, foreign reserves may have to be sold to help stabilise the currency, then the monetary policy has to sell Asian bonds, aggravating the crisis by depressing the bondmarket. This kind of procyclicality is something to be avoided in institutional design. The Asian Bond Corporation proposal does not have such a deficiency.

Table 3.7 shows a typical balance sheet of the Asian Bond Corporation. Here, the two currency examples are chosen for their simplicity. Suppose that the Asian Bond Corporation purchases 1 billion yen of Japanese government bonds and 200 million baht of Thai government bonds. Suppose that the initial exchange rates are 100 yen/US$ and 40 baht/US$. The total value of assets is US$15 million or 1.5 billion yen. Suppose that the Asian Bond Corporation issues 15 units of bonds, then one unit will be initially traded at US$1 million or 100 million yen.

Then, suppose that exchange rates fluctuate. Table 3.8 summarises possible cases of exchange rate fluctuations. In Case 1, both the yen and the baht depreciate against the US dollar, by the same percentage. The yen value of the ABC bonds does not change. In Case 2, both the yen and the baht depreciate against the US dollar, by 20 per cent. Again, the value of the ABC bonds in the yen does not change, although the value in terms of the US dollar appreciates. These two cases illustrate the point that is when Asian currencies move together with the yen, the exchange risk for Japanese investors is minimal.

Cases 3 and 4 illustrate situations where the yen and the baht move in different directions. In Case 3, the yen depreciates, while the baht appreciates.

Table 3.7 **Balance sheet of the Asian Bond Corporation** (two-currency example)

Liabilities	Assets
ABC sovereign bonds (15 units)	Japanese government bond (1 billion yen)
	Thai government bond (200 million baht)

Table 3.8 **Fluctuations of ABC bond values**

	Yen/US$	Baht/US$	Unit price of ABC bond (US$ million)	Unit price of ABC bond (yen million)
Initial exchange rates	100	40	1.00	100.00
Case 1	125	50	0.80	100.00
Case 2	80	32	1.25	100.00
Case 3	125	32	0.95	118.75
Case 4	80	50	1.10	88.00

Note: 15 units of Asian bond corporation bonds with underlying assets of 1 billion yen and 200 million baht.

The appreciation of the baht against the dollar and the yen will push up the value of the ABC bonds in terms of the yen. When the baht depreciates against the dollar and the yen, the value of ABC bonds in terms of the yen will decline.

With these characteristics, would Asian bonds be attractive to Japanese investors? So long as the Asian currencies move in tandem with the yen (or the Singaporean dollar), the ABC bonds will be attractive to Japanese (or Singaporean, respectively) investors. The coupon yields of underlying assets are denominated in local currencies, so that the coupon yield of ABC bonds will be a basket value of underlying assets.

Let us examine the possibilities of Asian corporate bonds. ABC corporate bonds can be issued just like government bonds. The Asian Bond Corporation should purchase corporate bonds that belong to the same risk categories (or credit rating) and have similar maturity and coupon payments structures. Corporate bonds should attract a wide class of investors since they carry higher risk and returns.

In the case of default (or non-payment) of bonds, legal procedures may be different from a country to another. This may be a substantial problem for investors wanting to invest in low-grade bonds. In some Latin American countries and Russia, government bonds were virtually defaulted. Corporate bonds are defaulted even in industrial economies.

Sovereign bond defaults pose particular difficulties, since they tend to result in a prolonged resolution process that may be marred by litigation against the country by minority bondholders. If changing terms and conditions is easier, say by a decision of super-majority (say 75 per cent), then a resolution process may be relatively easy. However, if changing terms and conditions require a unanimous consensus that may take a long time. Precisely this point led to the discussion of collective action clauses in the aftermath of the Mexican crisis of 1994–95 and the Brazil and Argentine crises from 1999 to 2002 (see Krueger 2001, 2002 for a proposal from the International Monetary Fund).

The Asian Bond Corporation: pros and cons

ABC bonds have the desirable feature of diversifying risk at the same time as offering reasonable returns. Investors in the low interest-rate economy will be attracted to the high-coupon rates of ABC bonds, if the currency risk is reasonable. Credit risk will be properly diversified, and informational asymmetry will be dealt with, since the Asian Bond Corporation will purchase bonds with similar credit ratings and provide information to investors.

Why not global?

One may wonder why investors are assumed to be regional, instead of global, in the Asian bond proposals. If bonds are issued internationally in New York or London, then the investor base is much wider, and the cost may be lower. This is a valid argument. If the government and corporations are reputable and highly rated so that they can issue local-currency denominated, international bonds with low premiums, then they should do so. However, not all Asian governments and corporations are held in such high regard. The view that the benefits of regional investment outweigh international investment is based on at least one of two related assumptions. Western or international credit-rating agencies and investors discriminate against Asian firms, for example, due to their credit rating being unfairly worse for Asian issuers compared to Latin American and central European firms. As well, investors in the region show more willingness to buy the bonds rather than international investors ('regional bias').

Asian investors are more interested in papers denominated in regional currencies than are international investors (known as 'home bias'). McCauley (2002) shows that about 46 per cent of 71 bonds issued by Asian institutions between April 1999 and August 2002 were bought by Asian investors in the primary market offering. Investors' familiarity with issues and correlations among the regional currencies are the basis of regional bias. For bonds denominated in local currencies issued by familiar regional brand names, regional investors will demand less premium than global investors.

A further point is that business hours overlap in the Asian region. Once an efficient trading and settlement system is developed, regional investors can enjoy real-time settlement in their business hours. This will be an additional benefit for investors in regional bonds.

Role of government

Lack of market infrastructure

Since the Asian region has fragmented financial markets, there is little common market infrastructure. The trading system is not coordinated between Tokyo, Hong Kong SAR and Singapore. Clearing and settlement may take time, since a common depository is not available. Bankruptcy codes are different from one country to another, so that investors are not quite sure what would happen should either default or bankruptcy occur. Protection of minority bondholders may not be a common practice. Standardised credit rating for regional companies is not available, as credit rating companies in the region offer only domestic credit ratings.

An Asian bond proposal should include plans to improve market infrastructure, without which any promotion of Asian bonds will find a severe constraint sooner or later.

In terms of providing market infrastructure and legal harmonisation, the role of the government cannot be overemphasised. Cooperation among the governments in the region is essential to the success of regional bondmarkets.

Government versus market

Some critics think that government's role should be confined to establishing legal and market infrastructure, while others regard it desirable and important that governments in the region cooperate in promoting Asian bonds by issuing benchmark bonds, harmonising regulation and taxation.

Unless foreign investors are active, the government will have less incentive to reform markets. Unless issuers are abundant, investors will not have the incentive to research, and voice what they see as obstacles. There could be a bad equilibrium (no investors because of no issuers; and no issuers because of no investors) and a good equilibrium (a deep region-wide market). Cooperation amongst the governments, as well as cooperation between the government and the investors, is needed to jump from the bad equilibrium to the good equilibrium. A government-led strategy is needed to improve coordination among investors and issuers.

In fact, pushing the agenda will hasten necessary reform in domestic markets. The current lack of market infrastructure suggests that potential benefits from reform and cooperation among regional governments are considerable.

Attractiveness to investors

Some market participants and economists question the attractiveness of ABC bonds.

Investors want to make decisions themselves on the basis of weights. ABC bonds are essentially mutual funds, or currency boards, in the sense that the values of ABC bonds are matched by the sum of underlying asset values. However, unlike mutual funds, assets in the basket are fixed in the beginning and not managed actively. Even international investors, who want to diversify risk by holding various currencies and various class of risk, would prefer to manage their own portfolio rather than maintaining a fixed-weight portfolio as the regional financial environment changes.

This criticism can be rebutted as follows, although there is some truth in the argument. The critics assume that investors hold only ABC bonds. In the real world, sophisticated investors hold many kinds of assets and ABC bonds will be only one of the alternatives. Investors will also adjust their portfolio according to their perceived business prospects. Investors will increase or decrease the ratio of ABC bonds relative to other regional or international currencies, so this point cannot be a criticism of holding ABC bonds. The issue will then be the benefits and costs of having a pre-packaged basket. Having pre-packaged assets (similar to the role of having derivatives) saves transaction costs. For example, suppose that investors would like their portfolio to weigh heavily on the Thai baht, relative to other currencies in the basket. Investors would buy the baht bond, and sell all other currencies (say Korean won, Japanese yen, Malaysian ringitt, Singaporean dollar and Indonesian rupiah). Buying additional baht bonds while selling the ABC bonds would mimic this operation. Conversely, the investor may like to shed a particular currency or a particular bond from the portfolio that originally contain ABC bonds. The investor does not have to sell all ABC bonds to get rid of the weak currency from the portfolio. The investor can simply sell forward the amount of the weak currency (bond) equivalent to the value in the component of the ABC bonds, while maintaining the ABC bonds in the portfolio.

So, the attractiveness of ABC bonds as a diversified basket product should rest on the savings to be made on the transaction costs of buying and selling the individual bonds together, just like a derivative. Given that domestic markets are not yet fully open to foreign investors and steady supplies of government bonds are not available, such costs would be very high.

Does the high correlation among the currencies provide more or less of a reason to promote the ABC bond? The regional currencies now show higher correlations among themselves than before. It was also the case, during the currency crisis of 1997–98, that the contagion effect made all currencies in the region decline simultaneously.

One view is that high correlation of the currencies in the region makes the ABC bonds less attractive, in the sense that it reduces the benefits of diversification. When investors seek a fully diversified portfolio, they should try to find financial assets that have negative correlation with most of their original assets, without compromising average returns. But this may not be possible in the real world. We do not find too much diversity in the portfolios of major institutions, and even less among small investors.

Another view is that high correlation of the currencies in the region makes ABC bonds more attractive, in the sense that those who are worried about currency risk may find the high correlation attractive, for example, risk-averse investors who exhibit home bias. ABC bonds may be quite attractive to these investors as the regional currencies move together.

The critics might ask whether these investors would be more attracted to a single-currency high coupon-rate foreign bond of a country with high correlation to the home currency. But suppose that the Korean won, the Thai baht and the Singaporean dollar have roughly the same correlation coefficient with the Japanese yen, then the diversification argument for these currencies still works. So, the high correlation of regional currencies is a plus for the Japanese investors when compared to other bonds, like the Canadian dollar or Australian dollar, while among the Asian currencies, with similar correlation coefficients, having a basket currency is better than the single currency. Another benefit of the ABC bond over a single-currency foreign bond is the diversification of credit risk.

Secondary market of ABC bonds

Since the value of ABC bonds will float against all currencies, the value will fluctuate against any of the regional currencies. When it is traded in Tokyo, the value will be quoted in the yen, and when it is traded in Hong Kong SAR, it may be quoted in the Hong Kong dollar or the US dollar. It all depends on the market facility and investors' preference.

Valuation of ABC bonds

The valuation of an ABC bond may or may not be a simple matter. Critics think that valuation would become so difficult that financial engineering techniques will be required to calculate the theoretical value.

However, the valuation would be straightfoward if the domestic markets for all underlying bonds in the asset side are deep and efficient. Then the value of the ABC bond is simply calculated in real time as the weighted sum of the underlying bonds. Any premium or discount that ABC bonds may show is the positive or negative value of pre-packaging them.

The valuation of an ABC bond may be difficult if domestic markets are not deep and efficient. In that case, the difficulty comes from calculating the potential market value of bonds with currency risk, interest rate risk and credit risk. However, this is a problem also affecting an individual bondmarket without sufficient liquidity. It would not neccessarily be the case that the difficulty in valuation would turn off institutional investors.

ABS Asian bonds

Some Asian bond proposals, in particular those from Korea, include securitisation of various kinds of assets. Asset-backed securities (ABS) can be issued for international investors. If distressed assets are to be securitised, it is proposed to separate senior debts and junior (subordinated) debts, and only senior debts are supposed to be marketed internationally. This is an application of a scheme that the Korean financial institutions are doing domestically (see Oh et al. 2003).

Critics point out that, first, distinguishing between senior and subordinated debts may be difficult. They are especially problematic if asset-backed securities bonds are marketed internationally in different countries, reflecting the difference in bankruptcy laws and implementation of asset collection. Therefore asset-backed securities bonds from different countries may not be packaged into a basket bonds, unless separation of senior and subordinated bonds is harmonised by regulation and the credit rating agencies.

Credit enhancement

In the immediate future, the number of potential issuers of Asian bonds may not be many, due to low credit rating. If a default probability perceived by investors deviates from a rationally calculated default probability of bond issuers, due to unfamiliarity or risk averseness, then there may be a role for the government or international institutions to enhance credit rating by provision of public money. Once familiarity is gained and history shows a better-than-expected survival rate, public support may be withdrawn. Such credit enhancement could be provided by the Japan Bank for International Cooperation or the Asian Development Bank.

Credit enhancement should not be a 100 per cent credit guarantee, rather, starting 50–80 per cent, with pre-announced schedule of declining ratio to 0 per cent within ten years. This will avoid the problem of moral hazard on the part of issuers, and will assure confidence on the part of investors.

Investor base

One may also question a list of potential investors. Bond investors are known to be risk averse, and Japanese investors particularly so, especially after the default of Argentinean Samurai bonds. However, Japanese investors' appetite for Samurai bonds issued by Bulgaria and Greece, in addition to Argentina, in the past show that they can take risk. Australian and Canadian bonds are also selling well, mainly due to high coupon yields. The spread of 4–5 per cent seems to compensate for exchange rate risk.

Singaporean and Malaysian pension funds (provident funds) may be other large potential investors in the region. They have an informational advantage on companies in the Southeast Asian countries, and may be willing to take risk for reasonable long-term returns.

Concluding remarks

An Asian bondmarket has the potential to become a major capital market in the region, providing that Asian governments realise the importance and cooperate in improving market infrastructure.

In order to provide better information and diversified risk, Asian basket currency government bonds can be constructed as bonds backed by a mix of local currency government bonds. The value of ABC government bonds is a weighted average of the values of underlying assets. When exchange rates fluctuate, the value of ABC bonds fluctuates as a weighted average of underlying assets. The coupon yield of ABC bonds is also a weighted average of underlying bonds.

Once the benchmark government bonds are created, ABC corporate bonds can be issued in ABC currency units. This provides an alternative channel of fundraising for Asian corporations. This provides high yield, reasonable-risk investment products for investors in the region.

Governments can help to develop such a market by providing credit enhancement in the early stages, and provide a suitable financial infrastructure. The governments of the region, especially Japan, Korea, Thailand and other willing Asian countries, are urged to cooperate in setting up the Asian Bond Corporation and promoting development of the Asian bondmarket so that the region can reduce reliance on the banking system, and help directly channelling saving in the region into borrowers in the region. The ABC sovereign bond may be created without significant changes to the current infrastructure; it is up to the will of the fiscal authorities. Securities firms will find investors who are willing to invest in a basket of local currency bonds with different coupons. The healthy development of capital market in the region will be important for the region in order to avoid another financial crisis in the future.

Note

1 See http://www.boj.or.jp/en/about/03/un0306a.htm for the announcement.

4 Institutional foundations

Credit insurers, asset-backed securitisation corporations and Asian bond funds

Michael Chak Sham Wong and Richard Yan Ki Ho

For the past few years, Asian governments have undertaken a range of measures to develop domestic bondmarkets, including issuing government securities, encouraging financial institutions to invest in marketable debt securities, implementing legal reforms for debt securities issuances, building infrastructure for bond trading and clearing, and establishing credit guarantee mechanisms. These measures are aimed at achieving financial disintermediation in national economies and diversifying the sources of public and private sector funding. While many arguments have been made as to the causes of the East Asian financial crisis, it is generally agreed that one fundamental cause was the global banks' collective withdrawal of their lending activities from the region. This caused some Asian financial and non-financial institutions to become insolvent, jeopardising the regional banking and economic systems. With the aim of making the financial systems of Asian developing economies less vulnerable, the International Monetary Fund, World Bank and Asian Development Bank have since actively promoted the establishment of domestic bondmarkets.[1] A domestic bondmarket can increase the efficiency of surplus funds allocation, retain domestic capitals, diversify funding sources for corporations and increase the number of channels through which governments can stabilise their financial markets.

The efforts that Asian—especially East Asian—governments have made to develop bondmarkets are evidenced by the growing size of their debt securities' issuances. China, Hong Kong SAR, Korea, Singapore and Chinese Taipei have made remarkable increases in bond issuance, with the total amount of their bond issuances in 2001 nearly double that of bond issuances in 1998 (Table 4.1). Due to global concerns about terrorism and economic downturns, bond issuance decreased in 2001. International and domestic capitals shifted to less risky assets, such as OECD government bonds and AAA bonds. In 2002, bond issuance in East Asia recovered and reached a volume close to its 1998 level.

In addition to bond issuance, many efforts have been made to promote the secondary market for Asian bonds. For instance, Japan proposed to build a regional bondmarket in Tokyo in March 2003. In late 2002, Hong Kong set up the Central Moneymarkets Unit to deal with clearing, settlement and custodian

Table 4.1 **Bond issuance and total financing in selected East Asian economies, 1998–2002** (US$ billion)

Total emerging market financing in East Asia[a]	1998	1999	2000	2001	2002
China	6,975.1	3,461.8	23,063.4	5,567.3	6,101.0
Hong Kong SAR	2,093.2	11,488.3	21,046.4	18,307.3	7,014.7
Indonesia	374.2	1,465.3	1,283.1	964.9	756.0
Korea	6,259.9	13,542.3	14,230.4	17,021.0	14,546.3
Malaysia	2,527.2	5,177.2	4,506.4	4,432.4	5,108.9
Philippines	4,113.0	7,181.7	5,021.9	3,658.8	5,797.3
Singapore	2,466.5	4,338.7	6,079.7	10,383.6	2,951.6
Chinese Taipei	2,439.1	4,019.9	6,703.5	3,794.0	9,279.0
Thailand	5,047.1	2,551.7	1,572.5	684.4	1,003.1
Total	32,295.3	53,226.9	83,507.3	64,813.7	52,557.9
Total bond issuance	1998	1999	2000	2001	2002
China	1,794.0	1,060.0	1,770.7	2,341.9	602.8
Hong Kong SAR	725.4	7,124.8	7,058.9	10,458.6	1,951.6
Indonesia	-	-	-	125.0	375.0
Korea	5,084.4	4,905.8	7,653.0	7,756.3	6,705.5
Malaysia		2,062.4	1,419.7	2,150.0	1,880.0
Philippines	1,890.0	4,751.2	2,467.3	1,842.4	4,773.8
Singapore	1,500.0	2,147.2	2,338.8	8,664.7	560.5
Chinese Taipei	1,041.0	475.0	1,698.0	2,152.4	5,450.8
Thailand	300.0	794.4	-	278.6	48.0
Total	12,334.8	23,320.8	24,406.4	35,769.9	22,348.0
Bond issuance/total financing (per cent)	38.2	43.8	29.2	55.2	42.5

[a] Total financing includes loan syndications, bond issuances and equity issuances.
Source: International Monetary Fund, 2003. *Global Financial Stability Report: market developments and issues*, March, International Monetary Fund, Washington, DC. Available online at http://www.imf.org/External/Pubs/FT/GFSR/2003/01/index.htm.

Table 4.2 **Size of selected capital markets, 2001**

	US$ billion				% of GDP				% of capital market			
	EU-15	US	Japan	Asian emerging market	EU-15	US	Japan	Asian emerging market	EU-15	US	Japan	Asian emerging market
GDP	7,906.9	10,082.2	4,169.9	3,229.7					15.34	18.50	7.65	34.72
Stockmarket capital	6,763.0	13,826.6	2,293.8	1,310.4	85.53	137.14	22.75	40.57	13.12	25.38	4.21	14.09
Debt securities												
Public	4,868.8	9,698.0	5,317.1	674.1	61.58	96.19	52.74	20.87	9.45	17.80	9.76	7.25
Private	6,974.6	8,806.3	1,608.0	595.9	88.21	87.35	15.95	18.45	13.53	16.16	2.95	6.41
Total	11,843.4	18,504.3	6,925.1	1,270.0	149.79	183.53	68.69	39.32	22.98	33.96	12.71	13.65
Bank assets	32,939.7	22,157.4	12,408.6	6,722.4	416.59	219.77	123.07	208.14	63.90	40.66	22.77	72.26
Capital market[a]	51,546.1	54,488.3	21,627.5	9,302.8	651.91	540.44	214.51	288.04				

[a] Capital market is the sum of stocks, debt securities and bank assets.

Source: International Monetary Fund, 2003. *Global Financial Stability Report: market developments and issues*, March, International Monetary Fund, Washington, DC. Available online at http://www.imf.org/External/Pubs/FT/GFSR/2003/01/index.htm.

services associated with trading of domestic and international bonds. A number of stock exchanges have allowed the listing of debt securities. Some investment banks have jointly developed electronic platforms for Asian bond trading. Do these activities reflect an active Asia bondmarket?

Is the size of Asian bond issuance sufficient? Does it have more room to grow? These questions can be answered by a comparison of the United States, the European Union (15 countries), Japan and emerging Asian markets. The size of Asian debt securities, including those of Japan, exceeds US$8,200 billion. This is 30 per cent less than the European Union and 50 per cent less than the United States. In terms of size of debt securities relative to GDP, for Japan it is around 69 per cent, for emerging Asian markets 39 per cent, for the European Union 150 per cent and for the United States 184 per cent (Table 4.2). Obviously, Asian bonds have much room to grow. In particular, the size of private sector debt securities in Asia deserves our attention. The size of private sector debt securities relative to GDP in Japan is around 16 per cent, and in emerging Asian market economies around 19 per cent. These ratios are far below the ratios in the European Union and the United States (both around 87 per cent). In addition, many of these debt securities from the private sector are debt instruments issued by financial institutions. Very few domestic corporations are able to issue debt securities in Asia.

Debt securities handled by the Central Moneymarkets Unit are denominated in euros, US dollars, Canadian dollars, British pounds, Australian dollars or Hong Kong dollars (Table 4.3). The list shows a very small number of debt securities issued by Asia-based corporations. Many of the debt securities are issued by global banks and multinational corporations. Data on fixed-income securities issued by Asian institutions are provided by HSBC, an active bond dealer in Asia (Table 4.4). Securities that have been issued and actively traded in the secondary markets are shown. Obviously, most of the bond issuers are governments and government-based corporations. Very few private corporations are represented, indicating that disintermediation in Asia, especially in emerging economies, has made little progress. Corporations cannot easily raise funds directly from lenders and must rely on bank loans to support their business. The bank loans are mostly short term or payable on demand. In the event of any economic instability, banks may collectively tighten their credit, causing debtor corporations to become insolvent immediately. In a worst-case scenario, this could lead to another financial crisis.

Table 4.3 **Issuers of the debt securities handled by the Central Moneymarkets Unit in Hong Kong**

Abbey National Treasury Services PLC
ABN Amro Bank NV
Agricultural Bank of China
AIG Finance (Hong Kong) Ltd
Airport Authority Hong Kong
Amoy International Treasury Ltd
Asia Commercial Bank Ltd
Banca Intesa SPA, Hong Kong Branch
Banca Nazionale Del Lavoro SPA
Bank Austria Aktiengesellschaft
Bank of East Asia, Ltd
Bank of Nova Scotia
Bank of Tokyo-Mitsubishi Ltd.
Barclays Bank PLC
Bauhinia MBS Ltd
Bayerische Hypo-Und Vereinsbank AG
Bayerische Landesbank
BNP Paribas, Hong Kong
Chekiang First Bank Ltd
Cheung Kong Finance Cayman Ltd
China Construction Bank
Citibank NA
Citic Hong Kong Finance Ltd
Citic Ka Wah Bank Ltd
Commerzbank AG
Commerzbank Aktiengesellschaft, Frankfurt
Commonwealth Bank of Australia
Cooperatieve Centrale Raiffeisen-Boerenleenbank BA
Credit Agricole Indosuez
Credit Lyonnais
Credit Lyonnais France
Dah Sing Bank Ltd
Dao Heng Bank Ltd
DBS Kwong On Bank Ltd
Deutsche Bank AG, London
Deutsche Bank Aktiengesellschaft
Development Bank of Singapore
Dresdner Bank AG
European Investment Bank
Fast Lane Investments Ltd
Fortis Bank
Fortis Bank Asia Hong Kong
GE Capital (Hong Kong) Ltd
Hang Seng Bank Ltd
HD Finance (BVI) Ltd
HKMC Funding Corporation (1) Ltd
Hong Kong Electric (Cayman) Ltd
Hong Kong and Shanghai Banking Corporation Ltd
Hong Kong Electric Finance (Cayman) Ltd
Hong Kong Mortgage Corporation Ltd
Hutchinson Whampoa Hongville Finance Ltd
Inchroy Credit Corporation Ltd
Industrial and Commercial Bank of China (Asia) Ltd
International Bank of Asia Ltd
International Bank for Reconstruction and Development
Jian Sing Bank Ltd
JPMorgan Chase Bank
Kookmin Bank
Lung Kee Investments Ltd
Malayan Banking Berhad (trading as Maybank)
Mizuho Corporate Bank Ltd, Hong Kong Branch
MTR Corporation (CI) Ltd
Nedbank Ltd
Nordic Investment Bank
Public Bank Berhad, Kuala Lumpur
Shanghai Commercial Bank Ltd
Standard Bank Asia Ltd
Standard Chartered Bank
Sumitomo Mitsui Banking Corporation
Sun Hung Kai Properties (Capital Market) Ltd
Swire Pacific Holdings Inc.
Swire Pacific MTN Financing Ltd
UBS AG, Hong Kong
UFJ Bank Ltd, Hong Kong Branch
Westpac Banking Corporation
Wharf Finance (BVI) Ltd
Wing Hang Bank Ltd
Wing Lung Bank Ltd

Source: Hong Kong Monetary Authority, April 2003.

Recent proposals for bondmarket development

In February 2003, China, Japan, Korea and the 10 member economies of ASEAN+3 agreed to develop an Asian regional bondmarket based in Tokyo (*Asian Wall Street Journal*, 3 March 2003, 'Japan proposes regional market for Asian bonds'). The purpose of the Asian regional bondmarket would be to prevent the occurrence of another currency crisis and stem the flow of surplus savings out of Asia. ASEAN+3 members have discussed a number of initiatives relating to bondmarket development, including

- active issuance of sovereign bonds by Asian governments
- allowing cross-border enterprises to issue domestic bonds to finance their foreign direct investments
- active development of the market for asset-backed securities
- issuance of bonds denominated in local currency, foreign currencies and currency baskets
- effective use of credit guarantees (such as Asian Regional Guarantees Facilities)
- developing the bondmarket infrastructure (accounting standards, disclosure rules, settlement systems, rating agencies, and rules and regulations concerning transactions).

Such initiatives would establish the framework for further cooperative efforts to be made by East Asian governments. However, an important question remains: can a regional bondmarket established in Japan, Singapore or Hong Kong really accelerate the growth of Asian corporate bonds?

A bondmarket mainly serves the functions of originating, underwriting, listing, trading and settling debt securities. Today, the first four of these functions can be performed easily electronically. Many financial instruments, such as equities, bonds and derivatives, can be structured, underwritten and traded in the over-the-counter market; they do not necessarily require a physical marketplace. The fifth function, settlement, may need to be performed in a market that allows free capital flows. In Asia, Japan, Singapore and Hong Kong could be good locations for bond settlement because of their free flow of international capital.[2]

The success of a financial market is not in its physical form alone, since many financial instruments fail to grow because of insufficient demand. Even as Asia provides the necessary infrastructure for bond trading and settlement, the region's corporate bonds will not grow if they are not of sufficiently good quality to appeal to international and domestic investors. Recent meetings of APEC leaders have identified two mechanisms to help improve the quality of Asian debt securities: credit guarantee and securitisation. This chapter extends

Table 4.4 **Asian fixed-income securities at May 2003**

Region / Issuer	Coupon	Freq. (US$)	Maturity to UST	Mid price	Mid spread
China/HK					
People's Republic of China	7.750	2	5 July 2006	115.58	2.494
People's Republic of China	7.300	2	15 December 2008	121.83	2.997
People's Republic of China	6.800	1	23 May 2011	121.27	3.644
China Telecom Hong Kong	7.875	2	2 November 2004	108.03	2.120
China International Training and Investment	9.000	2	15 October 2006	117.83	3.369
Citic Pacific Fin. (2001)	7.625	2	1 June 2011	113.52	5.513
CLP Power	7.500	2	15 April 2006	113.51	2.594
HK Land Fin.	7.000	2	3 May 2011	114.80	4.738
Kln-Canton Rail	7.250	2	27 July 2009	122.19	3.247
Kln-Canton Rail	8.000	2	15 March 2010	127.08	3.488
Hut. Wham Fin.	6.950	2	1 August 2007	113.81	3.372
MTR Limited	7.250	2	1 October 2005	111.46	2.195
MTR Limited	7.500	2	4 February 2009	121.90	3.247
MTR Limited	7.500	2	8 November 2010	125.35	3.588
Swire Pacific	8.500	2	29 September 2004	108.20	2.220
Wharf Capital International	8.875	2	1 November 2004	109.34	2.170
Wharf Capital International	7.625	2	13 March 2007	115.19	3.322
Indonesia					
Republic of Indonesia	7.750	2	1 August 2006	107.25	5.237
Bk Negara Indonesia	7.625	2	15 February 2007	106.14	5.761

Korea					
Republic of Korea	8.875	2	17 April 2008	125.19	3.19
Exp-Imp Bk Korea	6.375	2	15 February 2006	109.07	2.870
Korea Development Bank	7.375	2	17 September 2004	106.80	2.045
Korea Development Bank	7.250	2	15 May 2006	112.27	2.895
Pohang I&S	7.125	2	1 November 2006	112.47	3.244
Philippines					
Republic of the Philippines	8.875	2	15 April 2008	109.17	6.526
Republic of the Philippines	9.875	2	16 March 2010	113.85	7.166
Republic of the Philippines	10.625	2	16 March 2025	114.38	9.047
AC Intl Fin.	8.750	2	15 January 2005	104.65	8.169
Bangko Sen. Ng. Phil.	8.500	2	11 August 2004	106.73	2.752
Phil. Long Dist. Tel.	10.625	2	2 June 2004	104.65	5.809
Thailand					
Kingdom of Thai	7.750	2	15 April 2007	117.88	2.846
Ind. Fin. Corp-Thai	7.375	2	14 January 2007	113.83	3.296
Bangkok Bank (sub.)	8.750	2	15 March 2007	118.18	3.580
Malaysia					
Govt of Malaysia	8.875	2	1 June 2009	128.11	3.517
Malayan Bank (sub.)	7.125	2	15 September 2005	109.49	2.820
Petroliam Nas.	8.875	2	1 August 2004	108.08	1.870
Petroliam Nas.	7.125	2	18 October 2006	113.79	2.825
Petroliam Nas.	7.625	2	15 October 2026	115.69	6.329
Tenaga Nas.	7.625	2	29 April 2007	114.59	3.597
Tenaga Nas.	7.500	2	1 November 2025	109.47	6.679
Tenaga Nas.	7.625	2	1 April 2011	117.99	4.838
Maximum	10.625	2	15 October 2026	128.11	9.047
Median	7.625	2	13 March 2007	113.81	3.322
Minimum	6.375	1	2 June 2004	104.65	1.870

Source: HSBC markets, reported in *South China Morning Post*, 27 May 2003.

the discussion by suggesting institutional foundations required to ensure the emergence and growth of credit guarantee and securitisation in Asia. It also discusses the demand side of Asian corporate bonds and recommends the establishment of securitised Asian bond funds.

Credit quality of Asian corporate bonds

Many argue that the slow growth of the Asian corporate bondmarket is due to the lack of credit ratings on Asian bonds, due in turn to the reluctance of international rating agencies to analyse the creditworthiness of Asian corporations. Lack of information and insufficient demand for information on credit ratings may explain the inactivity of international rating agencies in Asia. Some argue that there should be more Asia-based rating agencies to provide credit ratings on Asian corporations. However, it could take years for such rating agencies to gain global recognition.

Let us suppose that many creditworthy and independent credit-rating agencies were present in Asia, and that these credit-rating agencies were actively rating Asian debt securities. Would this result in rapid growth of the Asian bondmarket? The answer is negative. High-yield bonds, previously known as 'junk' bonds, have been in the market since the early 1980s, and market growth over the past 20 years has been very fast. In terms of size, however, high-yield bonds account for only a small percentage of all debt securities issued. High-yield bonds represent bonds with credit ratings at speculative grades. They include emerging sovereign debts. In the bondmarket, investors are mainly institutions such as governments, central banks, supranational organisations, pension funds, mutual funds, multinational corporations, insurance companies and banking institutions, all of which tend to look for stable returns and have strong preferences on investment-grade debt securities. The bottom line of investment grade is Baa (Moody's system) or BBB (Standard & Poors' system) (Table 4.5). The Eurobond market mainly deals with assets of investment grade. The medium-term note market also deals with corporations or banks granted credit ratings or financial strength ratings at investment grade. Interbank transactions mainly involve assets of investment grade, which effectively act as a permit to gain access to a large pool of international investors.

The reality is that many Asian corporations find it hard to gain credit ratings at investment grade. Moody's credit rating on emerging sovereign debts in Asia—Singapore, Chinese Taipei and Japan—occupy the highest positions with double-A ratings and above (Table 4.6). Hong Kong SAR, Macau, China and Korea have only single-A ratings, and others have B-related

Table 4.5 Bond credit quality ratings

	Moody's	Standard & Poors'	Fitch IBCA	Duff & Phelps
Investment grade				
Highest quality	Aaa	AAA	AAA	AAA
High quality	Aa	AA	AA	AA
Upper medium grade	A	A	A	A
Medium grade	Baa	BBB	BBB	BBB
Speculative grade				
Lower medium grade	Ba	BB	BB	BB
Low grade	B	B	B	B
Poor quality	Caa	CCC	CCC	CCC
Most speculative	Ca	CC	CC	CC
Bankruptcy petition filed	C	D	C	C
In default	C	D	D	D

Table 4.6 Moody's ratings on Asian sovereign bonds, April 2003

	Government bonds		
	Foreign	Domestic	Risk category
Singapore	Aaa[5]	..	
Chinese Taipei	Aa3[5]	A3	
Japan	Aa1	Aa3[5]	
Hong Kong	A3[5]	A3[5]	
Macau	A3[5]	A2	Investment grade
China	A3	Aa3	
Korea	A3	Aaa	
Thailand	Baa3	Baa1	
Malaysia	Baa1	A3	
Philippines	Ba1	Baa3	Not investment grade
Indonesia	B3[5]	B3	
Vietnam	B1[5]	..	

Source: Moody's ratings (April 2003).

ratings.[3] The ratings on sovereign debts represent the lowest credit risk of the countries concerned. If a country has its sovereign debt at the bottom of an investment grade, its domestic corporations will struggle to gain investment-grade status and the bonds they issue will have to be sold on the high-yield bondmarket, where demand is limited.

Investors in the high-yield bondmarket have different risk preferences, and tend to look for high returns to compensate for the high risks taken. High-yield bonds in the United States can give investors returns both from bond yields and from drastic surges in bond prices caused by mergers and acquisitions. In comparison with high-yield bonds in the United States, Asian corporate bonds may not be attractive to investors. Also, the US high-yield bondmarket provides better information about corporate governance, better liquidity in the secondary market, more historical data for credit analysis and clearer legal protection for investors in case of insolvency. In short, to accelerate the growth of Asian corporate bonds, Asian governments need to lift the quality of these assets to investment grade.

On the supply side, let us suppose that many less risk-averse investors were prepared to invest in Asian corporate bonds. Would this result in the fast growth of Asian corporate bonds? The answer is negative. Yield spreads, representing the borrowing costs of bond issuers, for emerging sovereign bonds, high-yield bonds in the United States and investment-grade bonds are shown in Table 4.7. EMBI+ is an emerging market bond index developed by JPMorgan; it measures the borrowing costs of developing economies, mainly in Latin America. In recent years, EMBI+ has stayed at around 7.5 per cent. The Merrill Lynch US High Yield index measures the yield spreads of US high-yield bonds. It has stayed at around 8 per cent in recent years. Both

Table 4.7 **Yield spreads of emerging sovereign bonds and other bonds, 2000–2002** (spread in basis points)

	2000	2001	2002
EMBI+	756	731	765
Merrill Lynch US High Yield	871	734	802
Salomon Broad Investment Grade	89	78	62
US 10-year Treasury yield (per cent)	5.12	5.07	3.83

Source: International Monetary Fund, 2003. *Global Financial Stability Report: market developments and issues*, March, International Monetary Fund, Washington, DC. Available online at http://www.imf.org/External/Pubs/FT/GFSR/2003/01/index.htm.

emerging market debts and high-yield bonds are rated at speculative grade. If an Asian corporation issues bonds, its funding costs will be as high as 12 per cent (US T-bond yield, 4 per cent, plus yield spread, 8 per cent). Asian corporations with lower credit ratings may need to pay a yield of over 18 per cent. Will Asian corporations still be able to make profits with such high funding costs? Many Asian corporations are able to acquire bank loans at low interest rates of 5–10 per cent, thanks to collateral pledged with the loans. Poor credit ratings do not motivate Asian corporations to issue unsecured bonds.

Generally speaking, the availability of credit ratings does not necessarily facilitate the growth of Asian corporate bonds, since it does not increase either demand or supply. Ideally, there should be Asia-based rating agencies. But even Asia-based rating agencies would not be able to solve the immediate problem of an Asian bondmarket, especially given the length of time it would take to build brand names and reputations. Given the dominance of international rating agencies, a battle for dominance between regional and international rating agencies would so prolong the time needed to establish an Asian bondmarket that the market would lose its viability.

One immediate solution to the problem of Asian corporate bond growth is credit enhancement, which aims to transform Asian corporate bonds into investment-grade assets to suit the appetite of both international and domestic institutional investors. Most of the recent examples of credit enhancements fall into the categories discussed below.

Credit insurance and credit insurers

Credit insurance, or credit guarantee, can take the form of bond insurance, letter of credit, corporate guarantee or government guarantee. Bond insurance is widely used in the US municipal bondmarket. Municipal bonds are debt instruments issued by state, provincial and city governments. More than 50,000 state and local government units in the United States issue securities to raise funds for their infrastructure projects, schools, hospitals and other public purposes. Municipal bonds are subject to many risks, such as earthquakes, floods, tornadoes, environmental hazards and other natural disasters. To make municipal bonds attractive to risk-averse bond investors, interest payments and principal repayments are usually guaranteed by AAA-rated insurers. When an insured bond defaults, the insurer immediately makes the scheduled payments to the bond investors. In the United States, some insurance companies are deliberately established to serve as financial guarantors and credit insurers, and primarily insure municipal bonds and other debt obligations (Table 4.8). Many of them are active in the reinsurance market, where they swap and share credit insurance risks with other companies. These monoliners are regularly rated by credit rating agencies for their asset concentration, risk management system, management quality and financial strengths. In recent years, multiline insurance companies with several business lines have also begun to compete in the credit insurance market, thus diversifying their business and insurance risks. Some Asia-based insurance companies are also active participants in the business of credit insurance.

A letter of credit, also known as a bank guarantee, is a traditional form of credit insurance. Many top-rated banks guarantee their corporate clients in

Table 4.8 **Fitch IBCA ratings of US financial guarantors and reinsurers**

	Fitch financial strength ratings
ACA Financial Guaranty Corp.	A
ACE Capital Mortgage Reinsurance Co.	AA
ACE Capital Re International Ltd	AA
ACE Capital Re Overseas Ltd	AA
ACE Capital Title Reinsurance Co.	AA
AXA Re Finance SA	BBB
Ambac Assurance Corp.	AAA
Asian Securitization and Infrastructure Assurance Ltd	BBB
CDC IXIS Financial Guaranty (CIFG)	AAA
CDC IXIS Financial Guaranty Europe (CIFG Europe)	AAA
CDC IXIS Financial Guaranty North America, Inc.	AAA
Capital Guaranty Insurance Company	AAA
Capital Markets Assurance Corp. (CapMAC)	AAA
Commercial Guaranty Assurance Ltd (CGA)	AA
Connie Lee Insurance Co.	AAA
Financial Guaranty Insurance Co.	AAA
Financial Security Assurance International Ltd	AAA
Financial Security Assurance UK Ltd	AAA
Financial Security Assurance, Inc.	AAA
MBIA Assurance SA	AAA
MBIA Insurance Corp.	AAA
MBIA Insurance Corp. of Illinois	AAA
Radian Asset Assurance Inc.	AA
Radian Reinsurance Inc.	AA
XL Capital Assurance (UK) Ltd	AAA
XL Capital Assurance Inc. (XLCA)	AAA
XL Financial Assurance Ltd (XLFA)	AAA

Source: Fitch IBCA Ratings, April 2003.

their issuance of medium-term notes and bonds. In the past, banks benefited from offering their clients guarantees instead of loans, since this took credit risk off their balance sheets and reduced capital charges. This advantage has since disappeared, with current bank regulations' inclusion of bank guarantees in the calculation of capital charges. In addition to banks, well-rated corporations and governments can offer credit insurance or credit guarantee to bond issuers.

Credit insurance could be an efficient way of enhancing the credit quality of Asian corporate bonds. Although insurers would bear the credit risk, they could reduce their risk by overcollateralisation, diversification, reinsurance, securitisation[4] and other techniques.[5] The insurance premiums to be charged greatly depend on the amount of credit risk the insurers finally undertake. A top-rated bank can guarantee an Asian corporate bond by requesting collateral from the bond issuer for the guarantee provided, making the credit guarantee similar to a mortgage loan. In this arrangement, investors will enjoy a yield close to that of a bond issued by the bank, while the bond issuer will pay a yield cost close to that paid for a mortgage loan. However, insured bonds provide additional benefits. First, bond issuers can raise funds directly from the capital market, where more lenders and investors are present, potentially lowering funding costs. Second, issuers can gradually build their reputation in the capital market, a process that may lower their borrowing costs in the long run. Third, the insured bonds may reduce issuers' borrowing costs because of the lower liquidity risk undertaken by investors. Fourth, the insured bonds facilitate the development of a market with investment-grade assets. Fifth, a bank that has too much credit risk with a single borrower may transfer its credit risk to credit insurers, obtaining commission through the sale of credit business to the insurers. Such a mechanism enables banks to diversify their risk and rebalance their credit portfolios.

International, regional and domestic credit insurers

In order for Asian corporate bonds to be transformed into investment-grade assets, top-rated credit insurers and banks must be present in the Asian credit insurance market. In many cases, top-rated insurers do not offer credit insurance to bond issuers or debt obligators with very poor or no credit rating. In this case, governments, domestic banks or domestic credit insurers in Asia may offer partial or full guarantees on issuers,[6] thus making it more likely that top-rated insurers will insure them. The insurance premium involved will be shared by domestic insurers and top-rated international insurers. Domestic credit insurers can be government-sponsored institutions. For instance, many countries have established export insurance corporations and deposit insurance corporations. These insurers are mostly government-sponsored institutions operating on a self-financing basis.

Meanwhile, Asian governments can facilitate the emergence of Asia-based credit insurers. In 1995, the Asian Development Bank established the first regional bond insurance company in Singapore, known as Asian Securitization and Infrastructure Assurance (ASIA) Ltd. Ownership of this company came from financial institutions, ADB member economies, insurance companies and other organisations. In its early stages, the US monoliner Capital Markets Assurance Corporation subscribed 30 per cent of its capital. ASIA Ltd. primarily offers credit insurance to infrastructure projects of developing economies. In 2003, Fitch ICBA gave ASIA Ltd an investment grade of BBB (Table 4.8).

Once a sufficient number of top-rated, regional and domestic credit insurers are present, the reinsurance market should develop spontaneously. For instance, domestic insurers can insure a debt obligator for it to gain credit insurance from a top-rated insurer, while a top-rated insurer can reduce its risk by selling its stake in an insurance contract to regional and domestic insurers. An active market of credit insurance and credit reinsurance tends to result in rapid growth in credit derivatives and insurance-linked securities. These instruments provide effective tools for credit insurers and banks to diversify and hedge their credit risk effectively. With more tools to hedge credit risk, international investors, top-rated insurers and top-rated financial institutions will be more willing to take their stakes in the Asian credit market.

Asset securitisation and asset-backed securitisation corporations

Asset securitisation involves the pooling of many small assets into a trust (or special-purpose company), units of which are then sold to many investors in the form of asset-backed securities. Asset securitisation is frequently applied to debts, such as residential mortgage loans, commercial mortgage loans, credit-card loans, high-yield bonds, leasing revenue, credit derivatives (or credit insurance) and non-performing loans. It also applies to real estate, rent income, airfare revenue and telephone services revenue.

Securitised debts offer several benefits to investors. First, they allow investors to easily invest in a well-diversified portfolio composed of many debts. Second, they are mostly insured through a pool-insurance policy, in which an insurer bears the credit risk of the debts in the portfolio. Because of risk diversification and the attachment of credit insurance policies, securitised debts mostly gain credit ratings at investment grade.

Over the past few years, Asian securitisation has developed very slowly. In relative terms, Korea has been most active in Asia in 2000–01 in asset securitisation (Table 4.9). In 1998, Korea enacted a package of laws, known as the Securitisation Act, providing a simple and effective legal framework for asset securitisation, thus facilitating the securitisation of non-performing bank loans and the restructuring of the balance sheet of nearly insolvent corporations.

Securitisation of Asian corporate bonds

A simple way of transforming Asian corporate bonds into investment-grade assets is to pool them to become securitised corporate bonds. In the United States, collateralised debt obligation, which is a form of securitised debt, grew very fast after the mid 1990s. Collateralised debt obligation can include collateralised loan obligation and collateralised bond obligation, both of which are insured by pool insurance policies.[7] Collateralised bond obligations are securities backed by a pool of high-yield bonds; as such, they satisfy the market demand for high-yield assets with credit protection. Collateralised loan obligations are securities backed by a pool of bank loans. Issuance of collateralised loan obligations enables commercial banks to put their assets off their balance sheets and thus reduce their regulatory capital requirements.

Issuance of Asian collateralised bond obligations can drastically increase the supply of investment-grade debt securities in Asia. Because top-rated, regional and domestic credit insurers insure the cash flows from the bonds, collateralised bond obligations are safe assets. A large asset pool of collateralised bond obligations (CBO) can be listed and traded on the exchange or in the over-the-counter market. In 2000, Korea introduced the Primary CBO Guarantee Program via the Korea Credit Guarantee Fund. This collateralised bond obligation program fills the credit-quality gap between bond issuers and bond investors. The securitisation of Asian corporate bonds benefits many parties, namely the Asian corporations that issue the bonds, the originators that structure the collateralised bond obligations, the insurers that offer the credit insurance and the countries that obtain capital inflows.

Establishment of asset-backed securitisation corporations

Who should be an originator of collateralised bond obligations? Currently, international market players are reluctant to take a proactive role in Asian securitisation because the regulations that should protect their interests are still unclear. The Asian Bankers Association (2003) has suggested a number of ways to promote asset securitisation in Asia, including standardisation of contracts, development of secondary markets, development of the market for credit default swaps, and strengthening of mortgage origination, underwriting and servicing standards. To facilitate the growth of market forces in the long

Table 4.9 **Asset securitisation in Asia, 2000–2001**

Issue date	Region/country	Originator/issuer	Underlying asset
April 2001	Hong Kong	Commercial Plaza Sec Ltd	Commercial properties
April 2001	Korea	Credit Creator Ltd	Auto loans
February 2001	Korea	HAN LSP (KDB) Plc	Credit derivatives
January 2001	Korea	OZ Receivables	Air-fare revenues
December 2000	Hong Kong	HK Synthetic MBS Co. Ltd	Commercial properties
September 2000	Singapore	Pioneer Export Funding Ltd	Trading assets
October 2000	Hong Kong	Commercial Plaza Sec. Ltd	Commercial properties
August 2000	Multiple	United Asian CBO 1 Ltd	Loans and bonds
August 2000	Korea	HAN LSP (KDB) Plc	Credit derivatives
August 2000	Korea	Korea Asset Funding Corporation	Loans and bonds
April 2000	Korea	Sogeko Funding Corporation	Equipment lease assets
April 2000	Korea	KDBC Leasing Receivables 1 Plc	Equipment lease assets

Source: Ikeya, Makoto, 2001. 'Securitization market in Asia (excluding Japan) stalls: public commitment and initiatives to be tested', R&I Asian Focus Special Report, Ratings and Investment Information Inc., Tokyo. Available online at http://www.r-i.co.jp/eng/release/nr_international/asia010904.pdf.

run, Asian governments can take a lead in coordinating the development of the asset-backed securities market. Korea's Primary CBO Guarantee Program is a good example of governmental efforts in asset securitisation. Another example is Hong Kong's Mortgage Corporation, a subsidiary of the Hong Kong Monetary Authority, which deals with mortgage securitisation and operates on a completely self-financing basis. Asian governments should follow such examples and set up government-sponsored asset-backed securitisation corporations to deal with bond and loan securitisation. In the United States, most residential mortgage loans are securitised through government-sponsored mortgage corporations, while other debt obligations, such as commercial mortgages and credit card receivables, are securitised through financial institutions.

The proposed asset-backed securitisation corporations could deal with asset pools throughout the Asian region or within individual Asian countries, aiming to coordinate and facilitate securitisation processes. For instance, they could recommend changes in legal frameworks to facilitate asset securitisation, establish standardised procedures to acquire sovereign debts, corporate bonds and other assets into their asset pools, arrange pool insurance contracts with recognised credit insurers, and distribute asset-backed securities through investment banks and commercial banks. Meanwhile, they could strategically initiate asset-backed securities of different risk profiles, such as country-based collateralised bond obligations, industry-based collateralised bond obligations, Asian sovereign asset-backed securities and other asset-backed securities, to meet the diverse needs of domestic and international investors. An additional advantage of securitisation is that it can easily transform a pool of domestic securities into international securities, when currency swaps are included in the asset pools.

Asset-backed securitisation corporations could play the role of advisers and intermediaries in the market. This would accelerate the growth of investment-grade debt securities in Asia, and thus assist in retaining Asia's wealth in the form of individual savings, pension funds and provident funds.[8] It would attract international capital into the Asian market.

Investor base and Asian bond funds

Another issue related to Asian sovereign and corporate bonds is investor base. A successful bondmarket needs a diverse investor base to ensure diversity in its funding sources. For example, the US Treasury securities market is a successful market because it attracts a wide range of investors. The investor base for Asian sovereign and corporate bonds, on the other hand, is currently very narrow.

In recent years, the proportion of international investors in the US Treasury securities market has grown to around 35 per cent (Table 4.10). Domestic institutional investors, including pension funds, mutual funds, banks and insurance companies, remain dominant. The proportion of individual investors has remained unchanged at around 12 per cent for the past 20 years. Credit enhancement mechanisms, namely credit insurance and asset securitisation, should encourage increased participation of institutional and international investors in Asian debts. Meanwhile, Asian governments should explore ways to facilitate the participation of individual investors in the Asian bondmarket. One simple way to do this is to develop bonds of smaller value to offer to the general public.[9] Another way is to promote mutual funds that invest primarily in Asian corporate bonds. This would encourage the general public to invest in a well-diversified portfolio of Asian corporate debts.[10]

To facilitate the participation of individual investors in the Asian bondmarket, the government bond fund could be further securitised to become a closed-end or open-end fund. Such a securitised Asian bond fund could be sold both to the general public in Asia and to global institutional investors. Assets in the bond fund should be insured bonds and loans to minimise the credit risk for individual investors. A securitised Asian bond fund would dramatically enlarge the investor base for Asian debt securities. Also, it would become an actively traded asset in the market due to its large market capitalisation and large number of individual and institutional investors. This liquid bond fund would nurture relevant financial derivatives and thus help international investors and credit insurers hedge their credit and market risk in Asia.

Conclusion

Asian governments have made considerable progress in government bond issuances in recent years. However, very little progress appears to have been made in disintermediation. This is because, at this stage, Asian corporate bonds remain underdeveloped. The key problem for the Asian corporate bondmarket is its lack of credit ratings at investment grade. Without the status of investment grade, Asian corporate bonds will struggle to gain access to international and domestic institutional investors, and the growth of the Asian corporate bondmarket will be slow. Three key institutional foundations are crucial to accelerate the growth of Asian corporate bonds: credit insurance, securitisation and Asian bond funds. The first two would transform Asian corporate bonds into investment-grade assets, while the third would enlarge the corporate bonds' investor base.

Table 4.10 **Ownership of US Treasury securities, 1982–2002** (US$ billion, per cent)

	Total holdings (US$ bn)	Individuals (per cent)	Mutual fund/ trusts (per cent)	Banking institutions (per cent)	Insurance companies (per cent)	US monetary authorities (per cent)	State and local govts (per cent)	Foreign and international (per cent)	Pension fund (per cent)	Others (per cent)
1983	1,056.7	13.4	4.4	20.2	4.4	14.3	10.8	15.5	13.5	3.6
1982	886.1	11.4	7.3	18.2	3.5	15.3	11.6	17.0	12.7	3.1
1984	1,244.8	14.4	4.8	19.0	5.2	12.8	10.0	16.1	14.2	3.6
1985	1,444.3	11.9	7.0	15.7	5.6	12.3	13.6	15.7	14.6	3.7
1986	1,606.4	9.0	9.3	15.4	6.3	12.3	13.3	16.8	13.4	4.2
1987	1,714.5	10.2	8.7	13.8	6.3	13.0	13.3	17.3	13.8	3.7
1988	1,825.2	14.1	8.2	10.3	6.5	12.8	11.9	19.4	13.3	3.5
1989	1,950.5	12.5	8.2	11.6	6.4	11.6	10.8	21.7	13.3	3.9
1990	2,178.4	15.4	9.3	9.8	6.3	10.8	11.4	20.1	12.9	3.9
1991	2,461.6	14.0	10.7	11.3	7.4	10.8	11.3	19.3	11.4	3.9
1992	2,746.5	14.3	10.9	12.4	7.2	10.7	9.5	18.9	11.2	4.8
1993	2,988.5	13.8	11.2	11.5	7.8	11.1	10.0	19.9	10.8	3.8
1994	3,148.2	19.1	9.9	9.4	7.6	11.6	7.4	20.1	11.1	3.7
1995	3,310.3	16.6	9.8	10.1	7.3	11.4	5.3	25.4	10.1	3.9
1996	3,472.6	19.7	7.3	8.2	6.2	11.3	4.6	30.2	9.9	2.7
1997	3,467.9	16.8	7.3	8.5	5.1	12.4	3.7	33.5	10.4	2.4
1998	3,372.7	16.3	8.0	7.5	4.2	13.4	3.1	35.1	9.8	2.6
1999	3,298.2	19.9	7.5	6.2	3.7	14.5	3.0	32.8	9.7	2.7
2000	3,019.5	14.9	7.9	6.6	3.6	16.9	2.7	34.0	10.1	3.3
2001	3,016.2	12.4	8.9	6.3	3.5	18.3	3.7	34.5	9.3	3.1
2002[a]	3,218.4	12.0	9.0	6.9	3.6	19.6	2.5	35.4	8.8	2.2

[a] Estimates of Bondmarket Association.

Source: Bondmarket Association of the United States 2003.

Credit insurance and asset securitisation have been hot issues in Asia for the past two years. However, as highlighted by former vice-president of the Asian Development Bank, Myoung-Ho Shin (2003), Asia's markets for securitisation and credit insurance remain underdeveloped. To attract the presence of top-rated credit insurers in Asia, Asian governments should support the development of regional and domestic credit insurers, and these, in turn, would nurture the development of a reinsurance market and enable the growth of credit derivatives and insurance-linked securities. With more tools to hedge credit risk in Asia effectively, international investors, top-rated credit insurers and top-rated financial institutions will find it safer and more attractive to enter the Asian credit market.

Asset securitisation is another way to transform Asian corporate bonds into investment-grade assets. Government-sponsored asset-backed securitisation corporations should be established to facilitate asset securitisation. These asset-backed securitisation corporations could standardise the contracts or procedures for acquiring assets in asset pools, soliciting credit insurance contracts and distributing asset-backed securities. A crucial factor in the success of Eurobonds, medium-term notes and asset-backed securities in Europe and the United States is their standardised contracts or procedures for securities issuance. Standardised contracts, procedures and legal documents that have passed extended and consultation can reduce transaction costs and increase investor confidence.[11]

A solid investor base is another important factor in the development of Asian corporate bonds. An Asian bond fund supported by Asian governments will no doubt strengthen the demand for Asian corporate bonds, but it will not widen investor base in the long run. A desirable strategy is to securitise the government-based bond fund into a mutual fund sold to individual and institutional investors. Such a fund would invest primarily in insured debt securities, exposing its investors to very little credit risk.

In this era of globalisation, an Asian bondmarket needs to meet the needs of both international and domestic investors, all of whom are rational and able to make global comparisons. Asian governments need to ensure the supply of investment-grade assets if they want to build their bondmarkets, and credit enhancement is an immediate and effective way to reach this goal.

Notes

1 The International Monetary Fund and the World Bank co-published a handbook on developing government bonds (World Bank/International Monetary Fund 2001), while the Asian Development Bank offered training programs for central bankers on developing domestic bondmarkets in APEC member countries (Asian Development Bank 1999).

2 The trading of American Depository Receipts is settled via investment banks of the United States, meaning that it may not be necessary to have a centralised system for custodianship and clearing of Asian bonds.

3 Some Asia-based ratings agencies tend to give more favourable credit ratings to Asian sovereign debts; the fact is, however, that most global investors base their investment decisions on Moody's and Standard & Poors' ratings.

4 Many insurance contracts are securitised and thus transformed into insurance-linked securities. Through this mechanism, insurance companies can offload their insurance risks, which are taken on by investors in insurance-linked securities. If no contingent claims occur, the investors earn high yields. For more detailed explanations of insurance securitisation, see Borden and Sarkar (1997), Canter, Cole and Sandor (1997) and Latza (1997).

5 An insurer can hedge the country risk of its pool of credit insurance. Sharp rises in credit defaults in a country are generally linked to sharp falls in that country's equity index and exchange rates. The insurer can buy put options on a country's equity index or exchange rate to reduce the country risk involved. On the other hand, if the insurer wants to hedge the credit risk on a corporate bond, it can buy put options on the equity of the corporation that issues the bond. Alternatively, it can issue equity-linked securities to hedge its credit risk. Since 2000, equity-linked notes have become very popular in Hong Kong among both institutional and individual investors, indicating that the high demand for equity-linked notes is due to the high yields they offer to investors.

6 Some governments in Asia provide guarantee schemes to support the financing of business firms. For instance, Korea has set up a fund to guarantee the issuance of asset-backed securities, while Hong Kong offers partial guarantees to small and medium-sized enterprises to enable them to acquire loans from banks.

7 Details about high-yield bonds and collaterised bond obligations can be found in Barnhill, Maxwell and Shenkman (1998) and Goodman and Fabozzi (2002).

8 Singapore's Central Provident Fund invests mainly in Singapore government securities, which the government issues in spite of the fact that is has no need for debt financing, having generated fiscal surpluses since Singapore gained independence in 1965. This means that the Central Provident Fund is a dead weight in the government bonds market, since it holds 70 per cent of Singapore government securities but as a passive national custodian of pension funds is under no pressure to produce competitive returns for its members (Ng 2000). A similar situation occurs in Hong Kong SAR, where mandatory provident funds invest heavily in Exchange Fund Bills and Notes while the government has no need for debt financing. Such Asian provident funds could easily drive the growth of insured corporate bonds or securitised corporate debts if there were mechanisms to facilitate their presence in the region.

9 The Hong Kong Monetary Authority issues Exchange Fund Bills and Notes that are similar to US Treasury securities. Their investors are mainly institutional investors. In 2000, the Hong Kong Monetary Authority began to issue Exchange Fund Notes of smaller size (around US$7,000 per contract) to the general public, thus helping to enlarge the investor base of government bonds.

10 In 1998, the Hong Kong government intervened in the equity market to counterbalance the attacks of global hedge funds. The equities purchased were securitised in a fund known as the Tracker Fund. All the units of the fund were later sold to both institutional and individual investors. Thus, Asian governments can take proactive roles in asset securitisation so as to adapt sovereign and corporate debts to the investment needs of the general public.

11 In case of insolvency, the enforceability of financial contracts is subject to the jurisdictions concerned. Cross-border insolvency arrangements can be complicated enough to increase legal uncertainty even in advanced economies (Bank of International Settlements 2002). In certain developing countries in Asia, insolvency arrangements and contract enforceability are made extremely uncertain by the very small number of available procedures. Guarantees on emerging economies' corporate bonds provided by international insurers will offer greater comfort to international investors than relevant laws enacted in the emerging economies themselves.

5 The structure and characteristics of East Asian bondmarkets

S. Ghon Rhee

The definition of the term 'East Asian bondmarkets' is elusive at best, and so it must be asked, 'What is a regional bondmarket?' This question, in turn, raises a series of related questions.

- Is this a market geographically confined to the East Asian region?
- Do issuers, buyers, underwriters and market makers all come from the same region?
- Are regional bonds to be denominated in one of Asia's currencies or in a basket of Asian currencies?
- If they are denominated in the US dollar or the euro, are they still classified as regional bonds?
- Do we expect regional bonds to be rated only by Asian rating agencies? Do we expect regional bonds to be traded only in the region?
- Finally, does it make sense to pursue a regional program when the global financial community is becoming increasingly integrated?

Before these questions are addressed, a reality check is in order to make sure we have a comprehensive understanding of the current status of regional market activities.

Fact 1. From an examination of 71 bonds with a combined face value of US$41.2 billion, issued by Asian borrowers (banks, corporations and sovereign/quasi-sovereign issuers from China, Hong Kong SAR, Indonesia, Korea, Malaysia, the Philippines, Singapore and Chinese Taipei) during the period April 1999–August 2002, McCauley, Fung and Gadanecz (2002) report that 44–46 per cent of these bonds were purchased by Asian investors in the primary market offering. They further observe that Asian borrowers usually rely on affiliates of US or European investment banking firms for book-running and assembling syndicates of underwriters, and that larger issues and longer maturities are placed outside the region. They conclude that East Asia's bondmarket activities are far more integrated than is often perceived.

Fact 2. Singapore is a small but important part of East Asia's bondmarkets. The market activities of its onshore market for Singapore dollar-denominated bonds and offshore market (known as the Asian Dollar Market) for foreign currency-denominated bonds are useful in assessing the degree of regional integration of financial transactions. Until August 1998, foreign institutions were not allowed to issue Singapore dollar-denominated bonds in Singapore due to the Monetary Authority of Singapore's policy of discouraging the internationalisation of Singapore dollars. However, in order to promote Singapore as a regional financial centre, this policy was relaxed and foreign corporations allowed to issue Singapore dollar-denominated bonds in Singapore on the condition that the proceeds were to be used for economic expenditure within Singapore; otherwise, the proceeds had to be swapped for a foreign currency within Singapore. After the policy change, the total issuance of Singapore dollar-denominated bonds by foreign issuers increased to S$2.70 billion in 1999, S$2.57 billion in 2000, S$1.83 billion in 2001 and S$3.22 billion in 2002 (Figure 5.1).[1] A total of 27 per cent of the issuers were from the Asia Pacific region, whereas the majority of foreign borrowers were

Figure 5.1 **New issues of Singapore dollar-denominated bonds by foreign entities, 1999–2002**

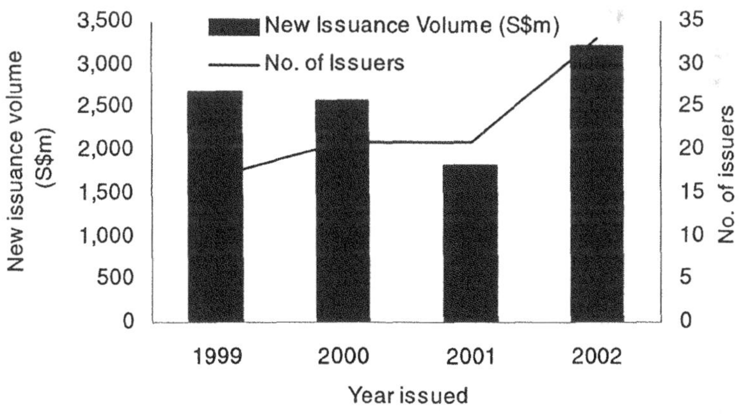

Source: Monetary Authority Singapore, 2003. *Survey of the Singapore Corporate Debt Market*, Monetary Authority of Singapore, Singapore. Available online at http://www.mas.gov.sg/singfinsec/download/2002DebtSurvey.pdf.

from the United States and Europe (Monetary Authority of Singapore 2003) (see Figure 5.2). While the bulk of Singapore dollar debt instruments issued by foreign borrowers were placed with onshore Singapore investors, the proportion of Singapore dollar debt bought by offshore investors increased from 1 per cent in 2001 to 10 per cent in 2002 (Figures 5.1, 5.2,5.3).

The total amount of offshore Asian Dollar Market debt issued in 2002 and 2001 amounted to US$10.9 billion and US$27.1 billion, respectively (Figure 5.4). At least 40 per cent of the borrowers in the Asian Dollar Market were financial institutions and corporations from the Asia Pacific region.

Figure 5.2 **Geographical distribution of foreign issuers: Singapore dollar-denominated bonds** (per cent)

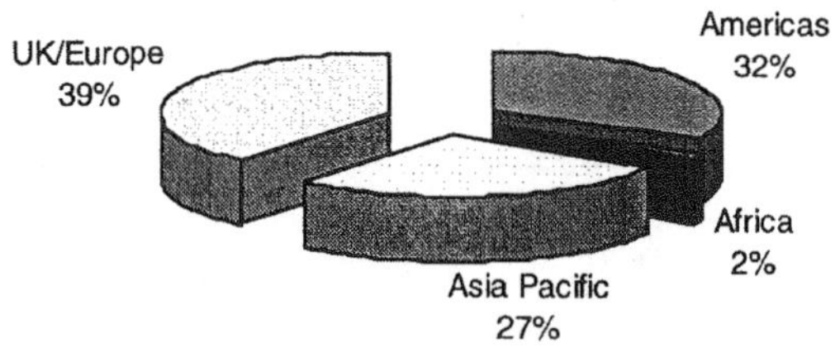

Source: Monetary Authority Singapore, 2003. *2002 Survey of the Singapore Corporate Debt Market*, Monetary Authority of Singapore, Singapore. Available online at http://www.mas.gov.sg/singfinsec/download/2002DebtSurvey.pdf.

Figure 5.3 **Types of foreign issuers of Singapore dollar-denominated bonds** (per cent)

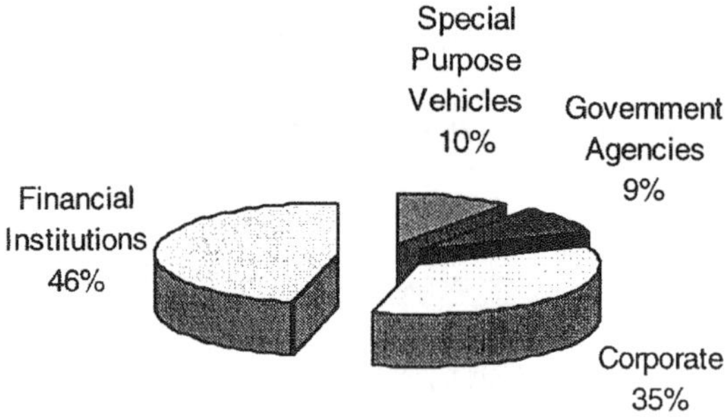

Source: Monetary Authority Singapore, 2003. *2002 Survey of the Singapore Corporate Debt Market*, Monetary Authority of Singapore, Singapore. Available online at http://www.mas.gov.sg/singfinsec/download/2002DebtSurvey.pdf.

Figure 5.4 **Non-Singapore dollar bond issuance, 1997–2002 (S$ billion)**

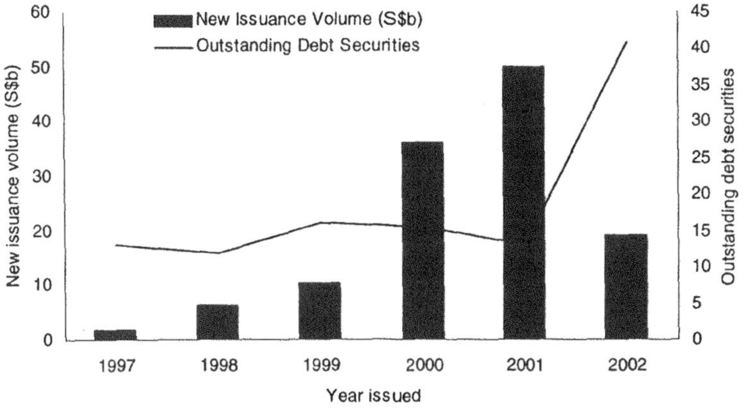

Source: Monetary Authority of Singapore, 2003. *2002 Survey of the Singapore Corporate Debt Market,* Monetary Authority of Singapore, Singapore. Available online at http://www.mas.gov.sg/singfinsec/download/2002DebtSurvey.pdf.

Figure 5.5 **Non-Singapore dollar bond issues, by maturity, 2001–2002 (S$ million)**

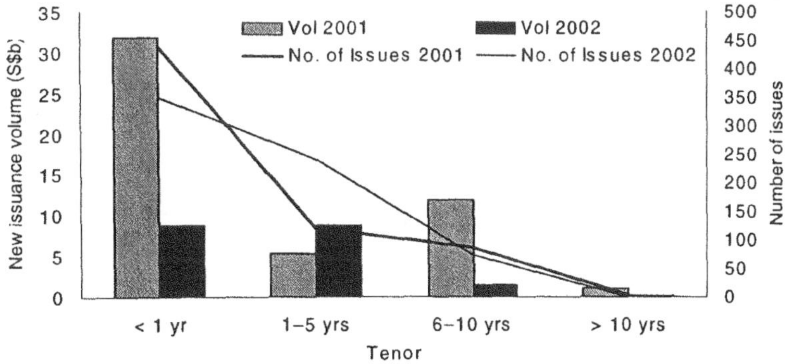

Source: Monetary Authority of Singapore, 2003. *2002 Survey of the Singapore Corporate Debt Market,* Monetary Authority of Singapore, Singapore. Available online at http://www.mas.gov.sg/singfinsec/download/2002DebtSurvey.pdf.

Approximately 92 per cent of non-Singapore dollar debt was sold to offshore investors. All debt issues in the Asian Dollar Market were private placements.[2] US dollars continued to dominate the Asian Dollar Market debt issues but its proportion of total amount of issuance declined from 92 per cent in 2001 to 76 per cent in 2002. Japanese yen and Hong Kong dollars followed with 15 per cent and 6 per cent, respectively. It appears that the Asian Dollar Market functions as a short-term market (mostly less than one-year maturity) for Asian financial institutions (Figures 5.4, 5.5, 5.6, 5.7).

Figure 5.6 **Types and geographical distribution of non-Singapore dollar issuers** (per cent)

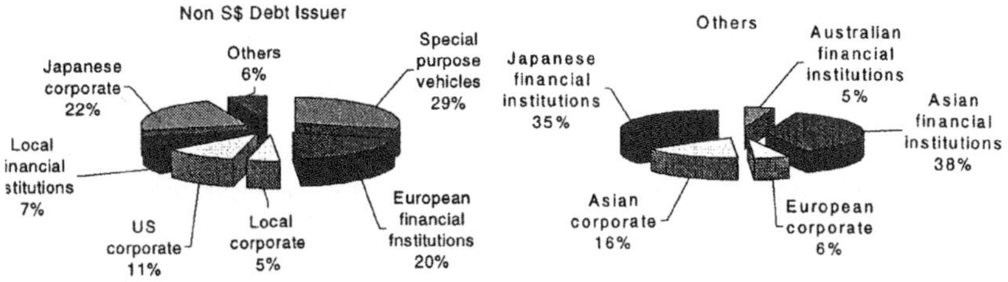

Source: Monetary Authority of Singapore, 2003. *2002 Survey of the Singapore Corporate Debt Market*, Monetary Authority of Singapore, Singapore. Available online at http://www.mas.gov.sg/singfinsec/download/2002DebtSurvey.pdf.

Figure 5.7 **Currency denomination of non-Singapore dollar bond** (per cent)

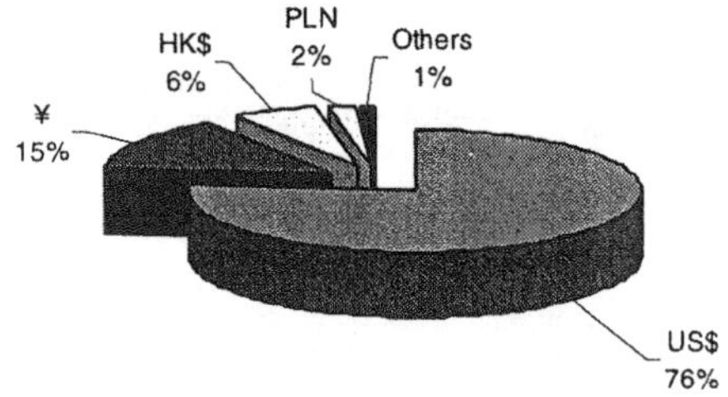

Note: Others includes A$, CA$, euro, £, NZ$ and STG
Source: Monetary Authority of Singapore, 2003. *2002 Survey of the Singapore Corporate Debt Market*, Monetary Authority of Singapore, Singapore. Available online at http://www.mas.gov.sg/singfinsec/download/2002DebtSurvey.pdf.

Fact 3. According to Bae and Park (2002), borrowers from six Asian countries (Indonesia, Korea, Malaysia, the Philippines, Chinese Taipei and Thailand) raised US$52.6 billion through bond financing outside their jurisdictions during the 11-year period 1991–2001. US and European investment banks served as lead managers for two-thirds of this amount and the remaining one-third was led by their Asian counterparts. The market share of Asian investment banks appears surprisingly large in view of the fact that 18 of the top 20 lead managers in the global investment banking business are US or European banks.

Fact 4. In the East Asian region, only Hong Kong SAR and Singapore are open to international bond rating agencies without domestic counterparts. All other Asian economies, including Indonesia, Japan, Korea, Malaysia, Philippines, Chinese Taipei and Thailand have their own bond-rating agencies. International accounting standards have been adopted for listed companies' reporting in most of the Asian economies, with the exception of China, Indonesia and Philippines (Table 5.1).

Fact 5. The Shogun bond (foreign currency-denominated bonds issued in Japan by foreign borrowers) market is Tokyo's offshore market, while the Samurai bondmarket (yen-denominated bonds issued in Japan by foreign borrowers) is the onshore market. Unfortunately, Shogun bonds have not been issued since 1994. The issuance volume of Samurai bonds peaked prior to the East Asian financial crisis in 1996 at 3.8 trillion yen, then declined following the crisis to 0.15 trillion yen in 1998 and 0.87 trillion yen and 1999. In 2000, the market recovered somewhat and Samurai bond issuance rose to 2.38 trillion yen, which was still below the peak pre-crisis level of 1996. Despite low interest rates in Japan, the issuance volume of Samurai bonds was only 0.64 trillion yen in 2002 (Table 5.2).

Fact 6. Dragon bonds issued by international financial institutions such as the World Bank and the Asian Development Bank are not liquid on the secondary market. Asian financial institutions buy these bonds on the primary market to take advantage of the withholding tax exemption and usually hold the bonds until maturity, raising questions about their contribution to the development of the region's bondmarkets.

The findings of McCauley et al. (2002) and the recent activities of Singapore's onshore and offshore bondmarkets indicate that Asian borrowers rely on US and European investment banks to tap global financial markets (mostly in London and New York), but that at least 40 per cent of these bonds end up in Asian portfolios. Why then is it so urgent to develop regional bondmarkets? This particular question cannot be separated from the definition of a regional bondmarket.

Table 5.1 **Regional bond rating agencies**

	Number of domestic CRAs	Adoption of IAS statements by SEs
Australia	Open to global CRAs	Yes
China	None	No
Hong Kong SAR	Open to global CRAs	Yes
Indonesia	2	No
Japan	3	Yes
Korea	3	Yes
Malaysia	2	Yes
Philippines	1	No
Singapore	Open to global CRAs	Yes
Chinese Taipei	1	Yes
Thailand	2	Yes

Source: Author's calculations.

Table 5.2 **Gaisai bond issues, 1991–2002** (yen trillion)

	Number of issues	Samurai bonds	Number of issues	Shogun bonds
1991	27	0.71	1	0.41
1992	37	1.57	-	-
1993	49	1.23	1	0.59
1994	60	1.26	-	-
1995	85	2.11	-	-
1996	154	3.79	-	-
1997	66	1.58	-	-
1998	10	0.15	-	-
1999	24	0.87	-	-
2000	63	2.38	-	-
2001	47	1.55	-	-
2002	29	0.64	-	-

Source: Japan Securities Dealers Association.

What do we mean by regional bondmarkets?

The creation of a regional bondmarket became a popular subject of discussion among financial market policymakers after the East Asian financial crisis of 1997–98. The single most dramatic element of the crisis was the abrupt reversal of private capital flows to the five crisis-affected economies (Indonesia, Korea, Malaysia, Philippines and Thailand) within a period of several months. In retrospect, however, the amount of the reversal—slightly greater than US$100 billion—was not too large for the region's economies as a group to handle. This amount accounted for less than 5 per cent of the combined pre-crisis domestic savings of the five crisis-affected economies and the five leading economies in the region (China, Hong Kong SAR, Japan, Singapore and Chinese Taipei) and only about 15 per cent of the total foreign exchange reserves accumulated by these 10 economies. Now that the accumulated foreign exchange reserves in the region are approaching US$1.5 trillion, or more than one-half of the world's foreign exchange reserves, the amount of the reversal which triggered the 1997–98 crisis seems trivial.

The region's policymakers have realised that had these savings been channelled into corporate financing without a reliance on short-term bank financing from outside the region, and had only 15 per cent of the accumulated reserves been allocated toward the capital account crises, the consequences of the East Asian financial crisis might have been very different. The former condition relating to savings mobilisation calls for the development of a well-functioning domestic bondmarket in each of Asia's economies, while the latter condition requires region-wide coordination on the systematic establishment of a pool of foreign exchange reserves available for an economy facing a similar capital account crisis.

In regards to the development of infrastructure for primary and secondary bondmarkets, remarkable progress has been made in each of the East Asian economies since the 1997–98 crisis. (See Appendix 5.1 for an outline of this progress with a focus on Hong Kong, Japan and Singapore.) The Chiang Mai Initiative proposed by ASEAN+3 finance ministers in May 2000 was a direct response to the call for regional cooperation on the mobilisation of foreign exchange reserves. Under this initiative, a series of bilateral currency swap arrangements among the ASEAN+3 countries is to be created, expanding swap arrangements of smaller scale that already exist among ASEAN members. However, the efficacy of this initiative has yet to be tested because of the potential overlapping of International Monetary Fund assistance programs. That is, the precondition for bilateral swap arrangements requires that the borrowing party should already be under or be about to come under the International Monetary Fund assistance program,[3] and the policy of 'strategic ambiguity' adopted by ASEAN+3 as well as by the International Monetary Fund and senior officials of the US Treasury makes it unclear how ASEAN+3 swap arrangements and the International Monetary Fund's supplemental reserve facility would be coordinated.[4] Such uncertainty and opacity simply add to concerns about the potential 'moral hazard' of the swap arrangements.

Where does a regional bondmarket fit in? We know that a regional market cannot substitute for a domestic bondmarket because a domestic bondmarket is one of three major vehicles for domestic savings mobilisation in any country, along with bank financing and equity financing. We also know that a regional bondmarket is one thing and a regional system of mobilising foreign exchange reserves is another. Now we have to think about exactly what we mean by a regional bondmarket. The narrowest definition of an East Asian bondmarket is represented by the union of the three circles signifying Asian issuers, Asian investors and Asian currencies. It may be expanded to include another circle denoting Asian investment banks. This produces an even narrower union of four circles. We may go one step further and require that all bond financing activities occur in Asian financial centres. Does it make any sense to pursue this kind of extreme regionalism? In reality, extreme regionalism comes at substantial cost. In the worst-case scenario, any effort oriented toward extreme regionalism will simply force all financing activities to move outside the region for lower-cost funding alternatives (Figure 5.8).

Figure 5.8 **Regional bondmarket**

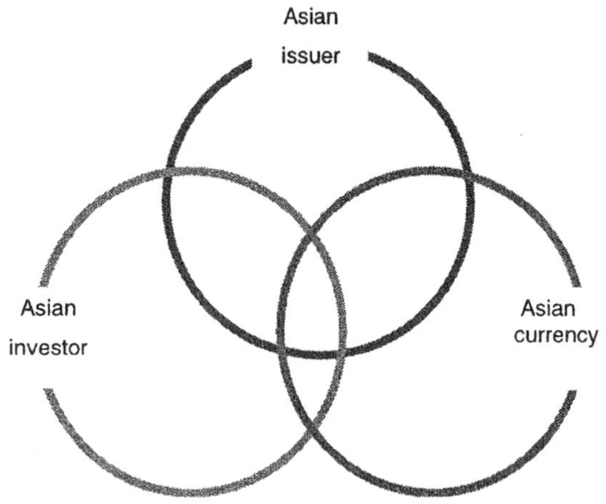

As long as Asian borrowers issue bonds at a minimum cost and the majority of these bonds are purchased by Asian investors, allowing them to gain the maximum yield, all other considerations are secondary. It does not matter where these bonds are issued, who rates them, who serves as the lead manager, where the bonds are traded or where they are cleared and settled. Given all this, the distinction between regional bonds and global bonds becomes either unimportant or irrelevant, because bonds issued by Asian borrowers in New York or Frankfurt can be purchased by investors in Asia. However, there are two major considerations that stand out and make the distinction between regional and global markets meaningful: credit enhancement programs and the Asian common currency.

Credit enhancement programs are necessary to assist Asian governments, semi-governmental agencies and corporate issuers that have received relatively low credit ratings from international credit agencies so that they can issue bonds at an affordable cost, if not at minimum rates (Table 5.3). So far, however, only minimal efforts have been undertaken by the region's economies to implement credit enhancement programs to facilitate bond issuance by Asian borrowers.[5] In a keynote address delivered at the ASEAN+3 High-Level Seminar on 'Fostering Bond Markets in Asia', Taniguchi (2003) suggested that the Asian Development Bank and the Japan Bank for International Cooperation provide credit guarantees to corporate and sovereign borrowers in Asia.[6] In a parallel paper, Rhee and Stone (2003) proposed that region-wide credit enhancement programs adopt the concept of municipal bond banks to gain the benefit of credit rating arbitrage and economies of scale by pooling the funding needs of Asian borrowers.

The creation of an Asian common currency and its use in denominating regional bonds has been widely debated, but so far very little progress has been made. The most significant development arising from the launch of the euro has been the integration of European financial markets. A strong convergence of short-term interest rates quickly created a liquid money market for the entire euro zone, while longer-term bondmarkets in Europe have exhibited some degree of market integration, as indicated by the decline of interest rate spreads among the 11 participating countries. The elimination of exchange risk, the harmonisation of market practices and the redenomination of government debt into euro-denominated debt have heralded the emergence of a bigger, deeper, more liquid and more homogeneous bondmarket for Europe (Quaden 1999, Duisenberg 1999). Similar advantages may be gained in Asia through full or partial currency unification as a result of common or partially shared monetary policies among the region's economies.[7]

Table 5.3 **Sovereign credit rating, June 2003**

	Local currency	Foreign currency
China	..	BBB
Hong Kong SAR	AA-	A+
India	BB+	BBB
Indonesia	BB+	B-
Korea	A+	A-
Malaysia	A+	BBB+
Mongolia	B	B
Philippines	BBB	BB
Singapore	AAA	AAA
Chinese Taipei	AA-	AA-
Thailand	A-	BBB
Vietnam	BB	BB

Source: Standard & Poors', June 2003.

Table 5.4 **Foreign holders of US Treasury securities, 2001–2003 (US$ billion)**

	March 2003	December 2002	December 2001
Japan	386.6	364.7	317.9
China	117.7	102.9	78.6
Hong Kong SAR	49.8	48.1	47.7
Korea	41.8	43.1	32.8
Chinese Taipei	34.5	34.5	35.3
Singapore	18.5	17.8	20.0
Thailand	13.3	16.3	15.7
Total Asia (per cent)	662.2	627.6	521.3
Total foreign (per cent)	1,242.5	1,204.5	1,040.1

Source: Department of the Treasury/Federal Reserve Board, 2004. Major foreign holders of Treasury securities, statistical table produced by Treasury International Capital System, United States Department of the Treasury, Washington, DC. Available online at http://www.ustreas.gov/tic/mfh.txt.

Recent proposals—the Asian Bond Fund and Asian basket currency bonds

With the region's combined foreign exchange reserves reaching US$1.5 trillion, the practical merits of diversifying the investment holdings of central banks in the region should be considered. At the end of March 2003, seven East Asian economies (China, Hong Kong SAR, Japan, Korea, Singapore, Chinese Taipei and Thailand) were holding US Treasury securities with a total value of US$662.2 billion, or 20 per cent of total outstanding US Treasury securities and one-half of total foreign holdings of US Treasury securities (Table 5.4). This amount is approximately 40 per cent of foreign exchange reserves accumulated in the East Asian economies, and the reserve holdings far exceed the requirements for exchange rate management or import coverage (Lim 2003). Two notable recent regional-level efforts in this direction are the Asian Bond Fund and Asian basket currency bonds.

In June 2003, the Executives' Meeting of East Asia and Pacific Central Banks (EMEAP) announced the launch of the Asian Bond Fund with an initial size of US$1 billion. The ABF will invest in a basket of US dollar-denominated bonds issued by Asian sovereign and quasi-sovereign issuers in all EMEAP countries except Japan, Australia and New Zealand.[8] The fund will be managed by the Bank for International Settlements. The EMEAP Group also indicated that it would review the extension of the Asian Bond Fund concept to include bonds denominated in Asian currencies.

Ito (2003b) proposes that an Asian Bond Corporation be established to serve as a depository for financial assets supplied by participating governments and to issue bonds that match the value of the assets.[9] The financial assets supplied by the participating governments would be local currency-denominated government bonds. In the second phase of development, the Asian Bond Corporation would be able to issue bonds that matched the value of corporate bonds denominated in various Asian currencies. The Asian Bond Corporation would function like a special purpose vehicle in an asset-backed securities scheme.

The concept of ABC bonds is simple because it borrows the idea of asset-backed securities, and it is intuitively appealing because it may serve as the precursor to an Asian common currency. While the Asian Bond Fund simply serves as a buyer of US dollar-denominated bonds issued by regional borrowers using the funds pooled by the region's central banks, the Asian Bond Corporation serves as an issuer of bonds that match the value of underlying assets denominated in government bonds and in various Asian currencies. When pooled, cash flows from pledged bonds (interest and scheduled repayment of principal) are distributed on a pro rata basis to the holders of the ABC bonds. Thus, the Asian Bond Corporation is effectively issuing pass-through securities. Although underlying pledged bonds are guaranteed by the full faith and credit of participating Asian governments, credit rating-related problems arise because not all governments enjoy the highest credit ratings from international rating agencies. Thus, credit enhancements will be needed even when government bonds are pledged. When corporate bonds are pledged as underlying assets, credit enhancements are a must, with two types being utilised—external enhancements and internal enhancements.

External enhancements include third-party guarantees, letters of credit and bond insurance. Third-party guarantees may be provided by official financial institutions such as the Asian Development Bank, the Japan Bank for International Cooperation and the Development Bank of Singapore. Letters of credit may be provided by leading commercial banks of international stature. A number of monoline bond insurance companies are in operation in the United States and Europe, which offer municipal bond insurance and pool insurance (Table 5.4).[10]

The most common form of internal enhancement involves the creation of senior/subordinated structures of pooled cash flows of pledged assets.[11] By restructuring the distribution of pooled cash flows, a new instrument called a 'collateralised bond obligation' is created.[12] Under the collateralised bond obligation scheme, two tranches of Asian basket currency bonds may be issued based on a pre-determined subordination level: senior bonds with higher credit rating and subordinate bonds with lower credit rating but higher yields. This type of structured bond issue became very popular in Korea in the post-crisis period (Oh et al. 2003).[13]

Although detailed operating procedures have yet to be designed for the Asian Bond Fund and Asian basket currency bonds, they do represent a good beginning and should draw the attention of financial market policymakers in the East Asian region to the need for credit enhancement programs and an Asian common currency. Another critical aspect which has often been overlooked is the liquidity of bonds on the secondary market. Neither the Asian Bond Fund nor the Asian Bond Corporation proposal can say much about this issue. With the Asian Bond Fund serving as an investment vehicle for the region's central banks, its immediate impact will be realised in the form of increased demand for bonds issued by Asian borrowers. The Bank for International Settlements, as an investment manager for the Asian Bond Fund, may end up purchasing US dollar-denominated bonds issued by Asian sovereign or quasi-sovereign authorities in New York, London or Singapore's Asian Dollar Market. Expected purchasers of ABC bonds include central banks and pension funds from within the region and institutional investors both from within the region and from the industrialised economies. Since central banks and pension funds are known for their passive investment strategies, it is possible that neither ABC bonds nor Asian Bond Fund-invested bonds will be instrumental in promoting market liquidity on the secondary market.

Conclusion

The creation of a regional bondmarket in East Asia can be justified for two reasons. First, it will facilitate credit enhancements for sovereign, quasi-sovereign, municipal and corporate borrowers. Second, it will facilitate the introduction of an Asian common currency. Without these two critical components, any efforts toward extreme regionalism are counterproductive and too costly to be rewarded in the global financial environment. Indeed, to confine primary and secondary market financial activities to the East Asian region would seem impossible, while to have only Asian homegrown-rating agencies provide rating services for bond instruments issued by Asian borrowers would be wasteful.

Appendix 5.1
Reforms for the development of domestic bondmarkets

With the banking sector still recovering from the recent crisis, Asian corporations have become less dependent on bank loans for funding and turned increasingly to capital market financing, establishing capital market reforms as an urgent policy agenda for the region's economies. Policymakers in these economies recognise that an active market in government-issued securities must precede the development of a corporate bondmarket. Many Asian economies have begun to accept fiscal deficits as necessary for the financing of bank restructuring and to adopt expansionary fiscal policy to cope with economic recession. Asian economies have therefore been reinforcing or creating market infrastructures to develop domestic government and corporate bondmarkets, thus laying essential foundations for the establishment of regional bondmarkets.[14]

Benchmark interest rates. The East Asian economies have demonstrated progressive attitudes toward improvement of benchmark yield curves. Traditionally, the lack of benchmark interest rates has been a major impediment to efficient pricing of financial assets and marking-to-market. For example, Korea has introduced a set of post-crisis reform measures, including consolidation of government-issued securities into treasury bonds to increase issue frequency and size, creation of the primary dealer system and elimination of arbitrary cut-off in determining winning bids in competitive auctions of government securities (Korea Securities Research Institute 2000). Hong Kong SAR, Malaysia, Philippines, Singapore, Chinese Taipei and Thailand have also concentrated on improving their benchmark yield curves either by extending maturities or by allowing the reopening of off-the-run issues to smooth out benchmark yield curves.[15] Artificial demand for government-issued securities under regulatory or statutory requirements was relaxed to minimise distortions to the benchmark yield curve. As a result, the captive nature of primary market activities has become less severe than in the past.

Expanding the investor base. Also observed in the region are some positive developments toward expanding the investor base for fixed-income securities. Philippines introduced a small-denomination treasury bonds program for individual investors to trade on the local stock exchange. In Hong Kong SAR, Exchange Fund Notes have been listed on the stock exchange since August 1999 to accommodate retail investors' demand for risk-free securities. In the past, individual investors were not eligible for direct purchasing of government bonds on the primary market in Korea; now, however, they are qualified to participate in non-competitive auctions. As such, a total of 20 per cent of each primary issue is reserved for individual investors in Korea. In March 2003, Japan launched government bonds tailored for individual investors.[16] Unlike conventional Japanese Government bonds, these bonds are redeemable one year after issue and have a minimum denomination of 10,000 yen and 10-year maturity. They carry a floating rate that fluctuates with the real rate of interest on a semi-annual basis. To promote holdings of Japanese Government bonds by non-financial companies, companies with capitalisation of 100 million yen or more will be exempted from withholding tax on interest income from Japanese Government bonds. Hong Kong SAR has launched a Mandatory Provident Fund to increase the demand for local long-term fixed-income securities by approximately 1 per cent of GDP per year consecutively for six years. Korea recently allowed bank trust accounts to sell employee retirement trusts. This represents a first step toward a corporate pension system.

Increasing supply of quality bonds. On the supply side of public bonds, positive developments are observed in the region. In the past, Singapore's statutory boards did not issue bonds because they had immediate access to government budget or commercial bank loans. When this policy was changed in 1998, a number of government agencies began issuing long-term bonds. Thailand's state-owned enterprises became major suppliers of high-quality bonds (almost 90 per cent of their bonds are issued under the government's guarantee), accounting for slightly over one-third of Thai public sector bonds. The Malaysian government, on the other hand, recently proposed the establishment of a financial guarantee insurer to facilitate the issuance of corporate bonds with credit enhancement.

Improving market infrastructure. East Asian economies have made remarkable progress over the past two years in creating and reinforcing market infrastructures in the primary and secondary markets for government bonds. Within the primary markets, competitive auctions have become the norm and foreign banks and financial institutions have begun participating in public auctions as primary dealers. To improve the efficiency of tendering and reduce delays, electronic bidding systems were introduced in Malaysia, Philippines and Korea. In order to promote competition among credit rating businesses, Indonesia, Malaysia and Thailand have allowed the establishment of second rating agencies; meanwhile, Hong Kong SAR and Singapore permit market entry to foreign rating agencies with minimal entry barriers. Furthermore, Hong Kong SAR, Indonesia, Malaysia, Singapore and Thailand have introduced a real-time gross settlement system for government-issued securities, while corporate bonds still need to advance to the level of progress achieved by government bonds. Korea, Chinese Taipei and Thailand are currently revamping their systems. Chinese Taipei has implemented a book-entry system for scripless trading in 1998 and all book-entry government bonds are settled through the real-time gross settlement system. Japan finally introduced a new scripless settlement system for government bonds in January 2003.[17] Although fixed-income securities are usually traded over the counter in the region, organised exchanges in Korea, Thailand and Indonesia have been creating their own trading systems to capture some of the over-the-counter trading volume. The Central Moneymarket Unit service was extended in Hong Kong SAR to non-Hong Kong dollar debt securities in 1996, and the linkage of the Central Moneymarket Unit with other central securities depositories in the region has since increased through a network of bilateral arrangements. Another important infrastructure project is the US dollar clearing system, which was fully implemented in December 2000. This clearing system facilitates the settlement of US dollar transactions in Hong Kong SAR and the wider region, and eliminates the settlement risks that arise when a transaction is spread across different time zones. With the Hongkong and Shanghai Banking Corporation Limited designated as the settlement institution, the system was implemented in three phases, with the first phase covering the US dollar RTGS system, the second phase facilitating payment versus payment settlement for foreign exchange transactions between the US dollar and the Hong Kong dollar, and the third phase implementing an interface between the US dollar RTGS system and the Central Moneymarkets Unit.[18] Through the operation of the Singapore Automated Clearing House, both Singapore dollar and US dollar-denominated checks are cleared in Singapore. Launched in July 1998, the Monetary Authority of Singapore Electronic Payment System settles scripless Singapore government securities on an RTGS basis. With its interface to the Central Depository of the Singapore Exchange, it provides for the settlement of Singapore dollar debt securities on a delivery versus payment basis.

Notes

1 Singapore dollar-denominated bonds issued by domestic entities are not included in the statistics reported. Singapore dollar-denominated bonds issued by foreign entities usually account for 10–20 per cent of the total Singapore dollar-denominated debt market.

2 The Monetary Authority of Singapore does not report a breakdown of Asian versus non-Asian investors.

3 Up to 10 per cent of the predetermined drawing amount could be disbursed without linkage to the International Monetary Fund facilities for a predetermined period—for example, 180 days.

4 The supplemental reserve facility is an additional borrowing facility where the maturity is shorter (one year as opposed to three years) and the interest rate higher than the usual facility.

5 Under the New Miyazawa Initiative, at least two measures were directly related to credit enhancement programs, that is, support for Asian countries in raising funds from international financial markets through the use of guarantee mechanisms, and possible establishment of an international guarantee institution with a primary focus on Asian economies. Unfortunately, there has been little follow-through on these programs.

6 The Asian Development Bank's current credit guarantee facilities are for project-specific funding purposes and although the idea of Japan Bank for International Cooperation's credit guarantee was floated in the New Miyazawa Initiative no progress has yet been made.

7 See Jang et al. (2002) for the implications of launching of an Asian common currency for the development of a regional bondmarket.

8 EMEAP Group's 11 members are Australia, China, Hong Kong SAR, Indonesia, Japan, Korea, Malaysia, New Zealand, Philippines, Singapore and Thailand.

9 Japan's Ministry of Finance also supports the idea of ABC bonds (Taniguchi 2003).

10 Recent communications with a leading municipal bond insurer, AMBAC, indicate that it has offices in London, Tokyo and Sydney, offering complete regional coverage of structured deals (not municipal or government issues) outside the United States.

11 Cash reserve funds or excess servicing spread accounts are common internal credit enhancement methods, but they are usually combined with external enhancement programs such as letters of credit and third party guarantees (Fabozzi et al. 1997).

12 Collaterised bond obligations are the same as the collateralised mortgage obligations introduced by the Federal Home Loan Mortgage Corporation in 1983 to expand the mortgage-backed securities markets in the United States. Collateralised mortgage obligations originally took the form of sequential-pay tranches with different maturities to appeal to institutional investors with preferences for instruments of different maturities.

13 One caveat is in order, for the collaterised bond obligation scheme simply reallocates risk between two tranches of ABC bonds; it does not reduce or eliminate risk. In a recent credit card industry crisis in Korea, the collaterised bond obligation scheme backfired to create potential financial risk in systemic proportion, forcing the Korean government to bail out the industry in April 2003.

14 For an overview of capital market reforms in the region, see Rhee (2000).

15 The regular issuance of Exchange Fund papers in Hong Kong SAR was substantially curtailed as of September 1998 to ensure that new issues of Exchange Fund Bills and Notes were fully backed by foreign reserves, in accordance with the discipline of the Currency Board system, except when there are significant inflows of funds. Beginning in June 1999, the Hong Kong Monetary Authority resumed issuance of 10-year Exchange Fund Notes and simultaneously reduced the issue size of short-term Exchange Fund Bills by the same amount, thereby leaving the overall size of the Exchange Fund Bills and Notes portfolio intact.

16 As of December 2002, Japanese Government bonds held by households accounted for 2.4 per cent of total outstanding volume.

17 Scripless settlement for corporate bonds has yet to be implemented in Japan.

18 With this system now in place, US dollar checks are settled in two days, rather than in two weeks as in the past (see Hong Kong Monetary Authority 2000a, 2000b).

6 The role of securitisation and credit guarantees

Hung Q. Tran and Jorge Roldos

A key policy prescription for the prevention or amelioration of financial crises in emerging markets is the development of local bondmarkets, a strategy that has been embraced by a number of policymakers and international organisations (see World Bank and International Monetary Fund 2001, 2003). From a macroeconomic perspective, local bondmarkets can soften the impact of lost access to international capital markets or bank credit by providing an alternative source of funding.[1] From a microeconomic perspective, they can help create a wider menu of instruments to deal with inherent currency and maturity mismatches in emerging markets (see Eichengreen and Hausmann 1999, Hong Kong Monetary Authority 2001).

Recent developments in Asian bondmarkets

Since the East Asian financial crisis of 1997–98, local bondmarkets have grown considerably in emerging market countries, and have gradually become an important source of funding for local sovereign and corporate borrowers. There is a widely held view that developing local bondmarkets can be an important means of reducing countries' exposure to maturity and exchange rate risks and 'sudden stops' in access to international capital markets. Local bondmarkets can also be beneficial in diversifying funding sources, especially for corporate borrowers, with their generally heavy reliance on domestic banks, many of which have been undergoing restructuring. In addition, improving local bondmarkets can help strengthen corporate governance and transparency, developing a credit culture in emerging market economies. As a consequence, the governments of many emerging market economies have actively taken steps to develop local bondmarkets.

There are regional differences in the recent development of local bondmarkets. In Asia, the need to finance budget deficits that emerged after the 1997–98 crisis, including the need to recapitalise banking systems, has given a strong impetus to the development of local government bondmarkets. In countries that have always had fiscal surpluses and therefore no financing needs (such as Singapore and Hong Kong SAR), governments have made a conscious decision to issue government securities to create a liquid government bondmarket, complete with a benchmark yield curve, as key building blocks to develop local bondmarkets. The weakness in bank lending has also contributed to some increase in corporate bond issuance, in Asia as well as Latin America. In Latin America, the strong growth of local institutional investors, especially pension funds, has created a growing demand for local bonds, while the corporate sector also has large refinancing needs due to difficult external financing conditions. In Central and Eastern Europe, the harmonisation of regulations (and institutions) in the process of accession to the European Union has stimulated the growth of local bondmarkets, among other things by attracting foreign investors putting on 'convergence trades'.

The total outstanding amount of bonds issued by Asian emerging market borrowers in both local and international capital markets increased rapidly to reach US$1.1 trillion at the end of 2001, slightly more than half of the total outstanding amount issued by all emerging markets (Table 6.1). Together, however, emerging bondmarkets account for just 5.6 per cent of the global bondmarket. Compared with other regions, emerging Asia has issued fewer international bonds (13 per cent of the Asian total outstanding), a larger but still not very dominant share of government bonds in local markets (50 per cent) and a large private sector share (20 per cent for financial institutions and 17 per cent for corporates). The composition of the Asian bondmarkets is thus similar to that of mature bondmarkets: domestic governments bonds account for 49 per cent of total bonds, financial institutions for 22 per cent, corporates for 11 per cent and international bonds for 18 per cent. By contrast, Latin America has issued more international bonds (32 per cent, mainly by sovereign borrowers) and government bonds in local markets (55 per cent), leaving a small share for the private sector (13 per cent). Similarly, countries in Central and Eastern Europe have also issued more international bonds (23 per cent) and government bonds in local markets (73 per cent), with a negligible share of 4 per cent for the private sector.[2]

The size of domestic bondmarkets in Asia, relative to GDP, is around 38 per cent, of which the corporate sector accounts for about 8 per cent. By contrast, the US bondmarket accounts for about 150 per cent of the GDP of the United States, with the corporate market accounting for about 24 per cent, while the

Table 6.1 **Size and structure of the global bondmarket, 2001** (nominal value in US$ billion)

			Domestic						International[b]	
			Government		Financial institutions		Corporate			
	Total bond outstanding	Per cent of world bond market	US$ billion	Per cent of total	US$ billion	Per cent of total	US$ billion	Per cent of total	US$ billion	Per cent of total
United States	17,598.2	47.3	8,557.1	48.6	4,367.4	24.8	2,452.5	13.9	2,221.2	12.6
Euro area 1[a]	7,861.5	21.1	3,210.4	40.8	1,751.7	22.3	355.4	4.5	2,544.0	32.4
Japan	6,104.0	16.4	4,439.8	72.7	713.8	11.7	693.2	11.4	257.2	4.2
Other mature markets	3,537.2	9.5	1,123.0	31.7	775.6	21.9	403.5	11.4	1,235.4	34.9
Subtotal	35,100.9	94.4	17,330.3	49.4	7,608.5	21.7	3,904.6	11.1	6,527.8	17.8
Emerging markets										
Asia	1,098.7	3.0	541.7	49.3	223.9	20.4	186.5	17.0	146.6	13.3
Latin America	694.3	1.9	384.4	55.4	67.4	9.7	23.4	3.4	219.1	31.6
Eastern Europe, Middle East, Africa	284.4	0.8	207.7	73.0	4.2	1.5	6.4	2.3	66.2	23.3
Subtotal	2,077.4	5.6	1,133.8	54.6	295.5	14.2	216.3	10.4	431.9	20.8
Total	37,178.3	1,000.0	18,464.1	49.7	7,904.0	21.3	4,120.9	11.1	6,689.7	18.0

[a] Euro area includes a total of 11 members of the Euro zone, excluding Luxembourg.
[b] Includes bonds issued by governments, financial institutions and corporates in international markets.
Source: Bank for International Settlements.

Table 6.2 **Emerging markets financing: domestic and international sources, 1997–2001** (US$ billion)

	1997	1998	1999	2000	2001	1997–2001
Emerging markets[a]	833.92	955.52	646.83	879.58	713.71	4,029.57
Domestic	669.89	865.16	545.55	741.41	609.84	3,431.85
Equities	37.28	32.70	43.42	25.50	19.02	157.91
Bonds	399.02	638.51	408.34	486.40	434.42	2,366.70
Bank loans	233.59	193.90	93.75	229.48	156.36	907.10
International	164.03	90.36	101.28	138.17	103.88	597.72
Equities	18.42	5.59	15.76	31.90	8.81	80.47
Bonds	83.25	48.37	56.97	54.50	60.23	303.32
Bank loans	62.35	36.41	28.55	51.78	34.84	213.93
Asia	238.88	268.86	308.76	396.05	395.77	1,608.33
Domestic	160.10	243.49	268.20	325.55	339.38	1,336.73
Equities	28.11	16.69	35.52	20.65	10.76	111.73
Bonds	6.85	42.70	46.71	98.41	147.75	342.42
Bank loans	125.13	184.11	185.97	206.49	180.87	882.57
International	78.78	25.37	40.56	70.50	56.40	271.61
Equities	10.50	4.05	13.92	26.45	7.65	62.56
Bonds	33.67	9.40	18.10	20.24	31.65	113.06
Bank loans	34.61	11.92	58.54	2,382.00	1,710.00	95.95
Central Europe[b]	50.68	79.21	63.17	61.72	94.86	349.65
Domestic	42.51	70.34	55.38	55.03	88.09	311.35
Equities	1.31	6.60	3.35	1.29	0.95	13.49
Bonds	43.43	47.59	59.78	56.94	65.08	272.83
Bank loans	−2.23	16.15	−7.75	−3.20	22.07	25.04

International	8.17	8.88	7.79	6.69	6.77	38.29
Equities	2.60	1.47	1.17	0.38	-	5.61
Bonds	2.53	4.65	4.48	2.09	4.07	17.83
Bank loans	3.05	2.76	2.14	4.22	2.69	14.86
Latin America	544.35	607.45	274.90	421.81	223.08	2,071.59
Domestic	467.28	551.33	221.97	360.83	182.37	1,783.77
Equities	7.86	9.41	4.55	3.56	7.31	32.69
Bonds	348.74	548.27	301.89	331.08	221.63	1,751.60
Bank loans	110.69	−6.35	−84.47	26.19	−46.57	−0.51
International	77.08	56.12	52.93	60.98	40.72	287.82
Equities	5.33	0.07	0.67	5.07	1.16	12.30
Bonds	47.06	34.32	34.39	32.16	24.51	172.43
Bank loans	24.69	21.73	17.87	23.75	15.05	103.09

[a] Emerging markets: China, Hong Kong SAR, Malaysia, Singapore, Republic of Korea, Thailand, Argentina, Brazil, Chile, Mexico, Czech Republic, Hungary and Poland.

[b] Incorporates sovereign issuance data.

Source: Capital Data; International Monetary Fund, *International Financial Statistics*, International Monetary Fund, Washington, DC; Standard and Poors'; Emerging Markets Database; and Hong Kong Monetary Authorities.

Japanese corporate bondmarket accounts for about 17 per cent of Japan's GDP. For Australia the share is over 10 per cent of GDP.

Asian local bondmarkets have become an important source of funding for both public and private sectors. In 1997, local bondmarkets supplied less than 3 per cent of the funds raised by Asian entities in all local and international loan, bond and equity markets (Table 6.2). In 2001, the share of local bondmarkets rose to 38 per cent of total financing, as the local bondmarket volume of US$150 billion almost matched the domestic bank lending total of US$180 billion. Over the same period, the share of international bond and bank financing fell from over 30 per cent to less than 15 per cent.

In Asia, the largest corporate bondmarkets are in Malaysia (equivalent to 51 per cent of GDP in 2001) and the Republic of Korea (28 per cent of GDP). Measures by Malaysia's Securities Commission to streamline the process of capital raising have supported further growth of the already deep corporate bondmarket. The cost of bond issuance has reportedly fallen below that of bank loans in Malaysia, and bond issuance has overtaken bank credit as a source of corporate funding since 1997 (see Moody's Investors Services 2002). In Korea, corporate bond issuance was concentrated among the major *chaebols*, guaranteed by commercial banks and placed with investment trust companies. These linkages led to the collapse of the bondmarket when a *chaebol* defaulted. The authorities have repeatedly supported the local bondmarkets through periods of instability since 1997–98.

Besides issuing more government securities, governments in many emerging market countries have implemented measures to improve market infrastructure, including the establishment of primary dealers. In particular, the Hong Kong Monetary Authority has continued to upgrade its trading, clearing and settlement systems, more recently linking up with Euroclear and Clearstream, and other local markets such as Korea in 1999 and China in 2002. Secondary market activity, as measured by trading volumes, has recovered strongly in the past years to exceed pre-crisis levels. The increase in secondary trading has been most noticeable in Malaysia and Korea.

Despite their relatively rapid development, Asian local bondmarkets still remain somewhat underdeveloped by the standards of mature markets, even though there is a wide regional variation in terms of size, depth, liquidity and sophistication. The main problem is that a modern bondmarket requires international best-practice in a wide range of inter-related fields so as to make them mutually reinforcing—from legal and regulatory framework to market infrastructure and foundation, to supporting markets such as repurchases and derivatives, as well as the presence of established investor bases. Weaknesses in one or two areas, despite progress elsewhere, can still cause problems for modern investors, causing 'the market' to move elsewhere. In fact, the main challenge of development, and not just of bondmarkets, is to attain a certain level of competence in a comprehensive manner. Specifically, the Asian local markets are illiquid, especially for corporate bonds. They remain segmented and insulated from one another, and in the case of China, even within the same country. In China, segmentation exists across investors, instruments and trading mechanisms. Investors in several countries are not allowed to invest outside of their home market, and international investors face difficulties and relatively high costs in hedging exchange risk when investing in local currency bonds. There is also a lack of standardisation across the region in bond contracts, underwriting, clearing and settlement rules and procedures, market regulation and taxation. Lack of transparency and lingering questions regarding corporate governance contribute to difficulties in pricing credit risk, helping to retard the development of a credit culture. Name recognition, rather than rigorous credit analysis, to some extent still influences investment decisions. Although the relatively large amount of government issuance has helped to establish benchmarks in local bondmarkets, it may have crowded out some corporate issuers. Moreover, for prudential reasons local institutional investors are often constrained in the range of instruments in which they can invest, which also reduces the available funds for corporate bonds.

It is important that authorities in the region continue to focus attention on implementing measures—in both primary and secondary markets—that can help further develop the Asian bondmarkets. In this context, the role of securitisation and credit guarantees has received much discussion.

The role of securitisation

Securitisation refers to the issuance of new bonds collateralised by a pool of assets, which can be other bonds, loans or any receivables with a regular cash flow. This is usually done via a special purpose vehicle specifically set up to own and receive the income from the pool of assets, and use it to service the bonds it issues in its name. The proceeds from the bonds issued are used to pay the original owner or owners of the pool of assets. The special purpose vehicle can be established by the original owner or owners of the assets, or by a third party.

The pooling of assets can provide diversification benefits to potential investors. Asset-backed securities can be issued in several tranches of different maturities and different risk–return configurations, and can be rated at different credit levels. Specifically, credit guarantees can be used to enhance the credit worthiness of some of the tranches, making them eligible to a wider range of investors. Credit enhancement can also be achieved through over-collateralisation of the asset-backed securities. Asset-backed securities can be issued in sizes bigger than those usually used in emerging corporate bondmarkets, and are therefore likely to have better liquidity in secondary markets—likewise desirable characteristics for investors.

Consequently, securitisation can contribute to the development of corporate bondmarkets by overcoming the problems of the small size and low credit quality of most emerging market issuers—problems that have plagued the emerging corporate bondmarkets. By participating in a securitisation program, or by collateralising their future receivable cash flows, small and medium-sized corporates are able to tap into capital markets. In addition, securitisation has served as an important tool for cleaning up banks' balance sheets and improving capital ratios during the bank restructuring process.

The best example of the use of securitisation to develop bondmarkets, improve access to low-cost finance and create overall economic benefits is the development of US mortgage-backed securities markets, which have surpassed in size the US Treasury securities market. Government-sponsored enterprises such as Ginnie Mae, Fannie Mae and Freddie Mae have played an important role in securitising diversified pools of mortgages and offering them to a wide range of investors—creating a stable and probably cheaper flow of financing to the housing sector, thus supporting the public policy goal of encouraging home ownership in the United States. These government-sponsored enterprises in turn have issued 'agency securities' to fund the purchase of mortgages, creating in the process a deep and liquid market.

More recently, the 'True Sale Initiative' in Germany has facilitated the establishment of a consortium consisting of Kreditanstalt fur Wiederaufbau and five commercial banks to securitise bank loans and offer them as asset-backed securities to a wide range of investors, including international institutional investors. This program is designed to help banks better manage their balance sheets, improve their capital ratios and eventually become more inclined to extend credit to the small and medium-sized companies that currently find it difficult to obtain financing.

Essentially, securitisation creates a derivative product assembled from existing (underlying) securities or other debt instruments. For the securitisation market to function properly, the market and market infrastructure for the underlying assets have to be in good working order. On top of that, legal clarity and predictability on things like the true sale of assets, taking possession of collateral and realising its market value also need to be sufficiently assured. Consequently, some analysts doubt whether securitisation can be used as a means to help develop bondmarkets, as a cash market has to be relatively developed before a market for securitised instruments can be introduced. In addition, to be viable, an asset-backed securities market needs to have in place institutions ready and able to provide credit guarantees or to buy the higher-risk 'mezzanine' tranches of the securitisation program. In emerging Asia, however, since bondmarkets have already been in existence for some time, albeit with large regional variations in terms of size, depth, liquidity and sophistication, securitisation can be useful in identifying gaps and deficiencies in cash market infrastructures and foundations. This in turn can help stimulate further reforms and developments in cash markets and beyond, in order to accommodate the proper functioning of securitisation markets (see Hong Kong Monetary Authority 2002).

In emerging Asia, Korea has the largest asset-backed securities markets, roughly equivalent to 45 per cent of the corporate bondmarket—not bad compared with a ratio of 59 per cent in the United States. The exponential growth of this market was triggered by the need to mobilise financing to address the problem of non-performing loans resulting from the 1997–98 crisis, and to restore liquidity to the banking system. Also helpful was the approval of the Asset Backed Security Law in 1998. In 1999–2000, collateralised loan obligations and collateralised bond obligations accounted for the bulk of transactions, as the focus was on addressing the non-performing loan problem and the refinancing of corporate bonds. In 2001–02, the focus was on securitising credit card receivables, the quality of which eventually suffered in the competitive rush for growth in the credit card business, with the Korean authorities having to step in to arrange rescue of affected credit card companies. Interestingly, even though residential and commercial mortgages have been securitised, they are not the preferred assets for securitisation as is the case in many other countries.

Recent experiences in the Korean corporate bond and securitisation markets, both in isolation and in relation to each other, are relevant in the debate about whether or how much securitisation—as well as credit guarantees—can help develop local bondmarkets. Corporate bonds were guaranteed by commercial banks prior to the 1997–98 financial crisis. They were concentrated in the largest five *chaebols*, and were little different from loans (only 17 per cent of corporate bonds were not guaranteed in 1996, compared with 97 per cent in 2001). They were then placed with investment trust companies owned, to a large extent, by the same *chaebols*. Waves of corporate defaults in 1998 and beyond have led to runs on investment trust companies. The government has had to step in to support the bondmarkets, as in current operations to support securitised credit card receivables markets.

Thus, although corporate bondmarkets have grown in volume, it is not clear how much this growth has helped improve the assessment and pricing of credit risk.

Thailand also passed a Securitisation Law, in 1997, but its asset-backed securities market has not visibly picked up. Market participants attributed this slow growth to the fact that, unlike the Korean law, the Thai law does not seem to adequately clarify certain issues critical to securitisation, such as the valuation and repossession of collateral, the legal status of special purpose vehicles and taxes. The Thai bankruptcy and foreclosure regime is also seen as inefficient and difficult to enforce.

The creation of a National Mortgage Corporation (Cagamas) in Malaysia in the mid 1980s contributed to the development of a deep mortgage market.[3] However, this market levelled off during the 1997–98 crisis, and has yet to pick up in a meaningful way—despite the approval of the Securities Commission Guidelines on asset-backed securities. Market participants note that while Malaysia's regulatory framework is favourable to securitisation, it is not as clear as the Korean law. Also, they note that the bankruptcy law does not appear to treat special purpose vehicles as bankruptcy-exempt (Dalla 2002). The lack of financial guarantees has been identified as a major constraint to the development of the market in Malaysia: banks and finance companies used to provide guarantees in 1995–98 with similar results to those in Korea. The authorities have since recognised the need for stand-alone financial guarantee companies, similar to the monoline insurance companies in the United States and elsewhere, and have studied measures to develop these institutions.

The financial centres of Singapore and Hong Kong SAR have well-developed regulatory frameworks for securitisation, but it is unclear how much this has contributed to the development of local bondmarkets. In Hong Kong SAR, the HK Mortgage Corporation has played a key role in developing a deep mortgage-backed security market, but issuance has slowed lately due to weakness in the housing sector. Some analysts argue that Singapore could play an important role in promoting securitisation at the regional level, through the establishment of a new regional credit guarantee corporation, or the revival of ASIA Ltd, the only regional credit guarantee corporation to have been established in Singapore (in 1995). A restriction on providing credit guarantees to non-Asian and industrialised Asian debtors is seen as the main reason for the corporation's limited success.

In Latin America, cross-border asset-backed securities are relatively more common than domestic ABS transactions, a situation similar to that of the region's bondmarkets. Cross-border structured finance products have been around since 1993–94, but issuance slowed down considerably in 2002 due to the financial turmoil in the region, which resulted in the first defaults on rated structured finance products in the emerging markets. By contrast, 2002 was a relatively strong year for domestic structured finance products (Fitch IBCA 2003a). Countries like Chile, Colombia, Mexico and Peru had banner years for local market securitisation. Much of the growth was driven by private sector pension funds, which are required for investment in instruments with high ratings, as well as by the increasing adoption of partial guarantees. The credit-enhancing effect of securitisation has allowed many issuers to access an otherwise closed market, further attesting to the positive impact of pension funds in local bondmarkets.

The role of credit guarantees

Credit guarantees or insurances protect bondholders against the event of bond issuers' default, or any other kind of mutually agreed 'credit event'. As a result, credit guarantees upgrade the credit quality of a bond issuer to that of the credit guarantee provider. Consequently, credit guarantees can be used to enable borrowers of low credit quality to access domestic as well as international markets. Providers of credit guarantees can be private companies, government agencies or international financial institutions. Credit derivatives markets also allow investors to hedge against default risk, in addition to providing a transparent pricing of corporate and sovereign default risks.

Private sector credit guarantees or insurance have been provided by monoline insurance companies for a long time in the United States. Since they became active in the US municipal bond guarantee markets in the 1980s, US monoliners have expanded their scope and now offer financial guarantees in international and emerging bondmarkets. In the past two years, US monoline insurance companies have come under pressure and several were downgraded as a result of the default of collateralised debt or bond obligations they had guaranteed. This has led some insurance companies to rethink their participation in this line of business.

In emerging Asian markets, the economics of providing credit guarantees to individual corporate issuers is not yet compelling. To become a viable business, financial guarantors must be able to insure a diversified pool of credits with a reliable and long enough history of default and recovery rates in order to correctly price the insurance premium. Failing these conditions, a financial guarantor can either not enter the business or must quote such a high premium that it would be prohibitively expensive for small and medium-sized companies to buy insurance and enhance their bond issues.

Given local corporate bondmarkets' small issue size and limited variety of borrowers, it seems more fruitful to think about providing financial guarantees at the regional level, where there are more opportunities for diversification. It also seems more feasible to arrange insurance for asset-backed securities, as the pool of underlying assets is already diversified to some extent.

In this situation, established international monoline insurance companies do have a competitive advantage over potential local companies, and they can provide added value to the development of local guarantees markets. Established companies will have compiled historical default and recovery rates for other regions, which they will be able to modify to use as a rough guide for the Asian market. Their involvement in local guarantees markets can serve as a training model for local firms.

Governments could set up agencies to provide credit guarantees to targeted borrowers, usually small and medium-sized companies in strategically chosen sectors. If these agencies do not charge commercial premiums, they actually provide a government subsidy to local companies. This in turn raises issues of transparency, fairness, potential for corruption and potential fiscal costs to taxpayers. Such subsidy may also be incompatible with World Trade Organization trade rules. In addition, they may relieve pressure for corporate restructuring, thus delaying the strengthening of the corporate sector. Finally, there is no reason why government agencies should be better than private companies in assessing credit risk—this, after all, is the key to developing a local credit culture.

Multilateral development banks such as the World Bank and the Inter-American Development Bank have offered financial guarantees to some emerging market borrowers, including Argentina (which issued a series of six US$250 million zero coupon bonds in 1999, maturing sequentially over 2000–04), the Electricity Generating Authority of Thailand (US$300 million in bonds issued in 1998) and Colombia (US$1 billion in amortising bonds issued in 2001). The intention of the guarantee program was to provide additional security to potential investors at a time when the issuer was having difficulty accessing international capital markets. However, guarantee structures such as the one used for Argentina (rolling reinstatable guarantees) are somewhat penalised in the markets because of the difficulty in modelling and valuing the enhancement incorporated in the bond.

In addition, credit derivatives markets also enable investors to hedge their credit exposures. However, in emerging markets, credit default swaps are currently only available for international bond issues by sovereign borrowers, and a few top-quality financial institutions and corporates.

Six areas for policy actions and reforms

Asian bondmarkets have grown substantially in recent years. Governments in the region should leverage this momentum to implement further reforms to bring the region's bondmarkets to a higher level of development. In the foreseeable future, the focus of policy will likely remain the improvement of local markets. However a longer-term vision of a more integrated regional market should be sketched, at least in broad terms, so that national reforms in policies and market infrastructures can be implemented with a view to facilitating rather than hindering the eventual process of regionalisation. For example, electronic trading, clearing and settlement platforms should be built with a view to them operating interactively across the region.

As a historical example, the development of European bondmarkets offers many useful lessons. Despite decades of gradual integration, including seven years of the single market, European bondmarkets experienced an increased degree of integration only when the euro was introduced at the beginning of 1999. The common currency has changed the investment practice of investors—some institutions such as insurance companies had faced restrictions on foreign currency exposures—and enabled the rapid take-off of corporate bond issuance. Even then, while money markets have been fully integrated, bondmarkets (let alone equity markets) are still segmented to various degrees, compared to the US market, due to less-than-perfect harmonisation in a variety of areas, including technical trading, clearing and settlement platforms.

Six areas of potential policy actions and reforms aimed at strengthening bond and securitisation markets in Asia are described below.[4]

Market infrastructure and foundation

In regards to market infrastructure and foundation, the following measures could be taken

- improvement of corporate governance and transparency, including accounting and auditing standards
- establishment of common financial disclosure and registration rules for bond issuers
- standardisation of bond contracts, underwriting standards and clearing and settlement procedures
- harmonisation of market regulation and taxation across countries.

Legal framework

An appropriate legal framework is particularly important for securitisation markets. In this regard, the following priorities must be set to strengthen contract enforcement and increase predictability in the resolution of contractual disputes

- increased clarity in the assignability of receivables and the definition of 'true sale' of assets
- clear legal status for special purpose vehicles—especially when they are used to securitise assets
- bankruptcy law and foreclosure practice
- clarification of data privacy and bankers' confidentiality.

Repurchase markets

A repurchase market that functions multilaterally for all market participants and not just bilaterally between commercial banks and the central bank can facilitate market participants' funding and liquidity management. This, in turn, can help improve bond underwriting, trading and management activities, leading to better liquidity in the secondary market.

Derivatives markets

Regulation (including disclosure requirements) and supervision systems must be put in place to encourage the development of financial derivatives markets so that market participants can hedge their interest rate, foreign exchange and credit risks. Credit derivatives markets are also useful in improving the efficiency of price discovery in local bondmarkets.

Investor bases

Asia needs to develop a more diversified range of institutional investors to complement the banks. In this regard, the following points are relevant.

- Experiences from Chile, Mexico and other Latin American countries that have implemented pension reforms show that pension funds, with their continually growing assets and demand for securities, can play a key role in developing local bondmarkets, increasing their depth and stability.
- Mutual funds are wonderful instruments for mobilising household savings and channelling them to capital markets. Experiences in Brazil, where a thriving domestic mutual fund industry has gathered more than US$150 billion in assets under management (or 30 per cent of GDP), suggest that the mutual funds can play an important role in developing, and bringing stability to, local bondmarkets.
- Restrictions imposed on institutional investors need to be eased to allow them to have a fuller impact on local markets.

- Capital controls need to be gradually dismantled so that non-resident investors both within and outside the region can participate in local markets.

Credit culture

Credit culture is an intangible but crucial ingredient that marks the maturity of a bondmarket. The following steps must be prioritised.

- Protection of creditors' rights must be ensured.
- The requirement that all bond issuers be rated by a credit rating agency must be adopted.
- A competitive environment for established international credit rating agencies and local agencies must be maintained over the long term. Again, experiences in Chile over the past 20 years show that such an environment is conducive to the formation of local agencies with a high degree of professionalism and credibility—a sign of the maturity of Chile's credit culture.

Concluding remarks

Local bondmarkets are gradually but steadily becoming an alternative source of funding for sovereigns and corporate borrowers in emerging Asia. To some degree, existing corporate bondmarkets served as an alternative source of finance in Hong Kong SAR, Korea and Malaysia after the 1997–98 financial crises. Progress in these and other markets over the past five years has meant that these markets are likely to buffer the impact of future disruptions in other financial markets. The rapid growth of local bond issuance, aided by the use of guarantees and securitisation, is substituting for the reduced access to international capital markets, but mostly for top-tier corporates. Analysts hope that measures to encourage the growth of private pension funds and other institutional investors, combined with the support of more transparent government benchmarks and better corporate governance and transparency, may extend the benefits of corporate bondmarkets to lower-tier credits.

Finally, the recently launched Asian Bond Fund initiative is likely to provide an additional push to the development of local bondmarkets. Even though the immediate direct impact of the Asian Bond Fund is likely to be modest, given its small size and the fact that international dollar bonds issued by Asian sovereign borrowers—the current investment target of the fund—already enjoy a strong local bid, its symbolic meaning is significant. It is further concrete evidence of regional cooperation on development of regional financial markets. Managed by a third party of sterling reputation—the Bank for International Settlements—and having transparent investment policy and guidelines, the Asian Bond Fund can serve as a tool for exerting peer pressure to ensure that best practices are adopted in the development of bondmarkets. This role will become even more relevant when the Asian Bond Fund eventually contemplates investments in local currency bonds.

Notes

1 See Greenspan (1999). However, while bondmarkets and banks have served as backup forms of financial intermediation in the United States, empirical evidence for a broader set of countries shows a positive correlation between bank lending and bond issuance (see HKMA 2001).

2 For a detailed discussion of emerging local bondmarkets, see International Monetary Fund (2002).

3 Malaysia's National Mortgage Corporation (Cagamas) was set up in 1986, with the principal aim of purchasing housing loans from financial institutions, funded by the issuance of fixed and floating rate bonds (Hohensee 2001).

4 A more general discussion for all emerging markets can be found in International Monetary Fund (2003).

7 The Asian Bond Bank

A good idea for credit enhancement

S. Ghon Rhee and Gregory R. Stone

The rate of interest paid by borrowers is dependent upon the structure of the loan and the creditworthiness of the borrower. The structure of the loan is often determined endogenously, whereas the credit rating tends to be determined exogenously. Several methods of enhancing credit ratings exist. This chapter discusses one of the most frequently overlooked methods, the bond bank.

Municipal bond banks first appeared in Canada in 1956 and in the United States in 1970 for the express purpose of lowering the cost of debt for municipalities. Since that time, municipal bond banks have been offering a unique and advantageous way for small communities to finance municipal projects. It is argued that a similar model could be applied to enhance credit ratings and reduce borrowing costs for Asian governments.

In the United States and Canada, many small municipalities lack knowledge about financial markets and need to borrow relatively small amounts of capital. The process of hiring an investment bank and floating a small amount of what will be an illiquid, and possibly unrated debt issue, can significantly increase the cost of borrowing for the municipality. Historical, structural and current financial problems have contributed to low credit ratings in many Asian countries. The enhancement of credit ratings results in lower borrowing costs, thus improving growth and wealth. In the United States and Canada, small or poorly rated municipalities face similar borrowing problems. One improvement available to many municipalities is the municipal bond bank. Municipal bond banks operate as credit enhancing organisations by 'pooling' multiple municipalities' borrowing needs into a single bond bank debt issuance, thereby modifying two important characteristics of the municipalities' debt.

Table 7.1 **Sovereign credit rating**

	Local currency	Foreign currency
China	-	BBB
Hong Kong SAR	AA-	A+
India	BB+	BBB
Indonesia	BB+	B
Korea	A+	A
Malaysia	A+	BBB+
Mongolia	B	B
Philippines	BBB	BB
Singapore	AAA	AAA
Chinese Taipei	AA-	AA
Thailand	A-	BBB
Vietnam	BB	BB

Source: Standard & Poors', June 2003.

First, the credit rating associated with the debt is changed. Municipal bond banks must have strong credit ratings if they are to fulfill the purpose for which they are intended. Bond banks operate by re-lending the funds obtained with their higher credit rating to the municipalities with lower credit ratings. This process is called 'credit-rating arbitrage', and is considered useful for East Asian economies (Table 7.1).

The second characteristic modified by municipal bond bank debt issuance is the size of the issue. By pooling the borrowing needs of multiple municipalities, municipal bond banks are able to offer larger debt issues, which typically make the primary market offering more competitive. With more competition in the primary market, one expects the price of the bond to rise and the municipality's debt servicing cost to fall. Savings are also realised through a reduction in the transaction costs associated with the economies of scale in the underwriting process. Savings from the anticipation of increased liquidity in the secondary market, due to the increased size of the offering, may also occur. Municipal bond banks typically offer professional management and minimal administrative costs to their members. Increased size and liquidity may benefit the smaller Asian economies or economies which infrequently or irregularly issue debt.

At least three empirical studies have attempted to quantify the impact municipal bond banks have had on US municipalities' borrowing costs (Cole and Millar 1982, Katzman 1980, Kidwell and Rogowski 1983). These studies have indicated that municipalities with credit ratings below that of the regional municipal bond bank realised savings from both an improvement in their credit rating and the economies of scale associated with the underwriting process. Municipalities with credit ratings equivalent to the municipal bond bank typically realised no savings from credit rating arbitrage, but did save in the underwriting process. Municipalities with credit ratings higher than the municipal bond bank realised no benefits from bond bank participation.

Unlike most governmental organisations, municipal bond banks have helped municipalities without imposing a financial burden upon the taxpayer. Most municipal bond banks operate efficiently enough to reduce the municipality's cost of debt while simultaneously paying for their own operations. The bond bank of Alaska has produced excess returns to the state every year since 1977 for a cumulative US$23.2 million (Alaska Bond Bank 2001). This sum is more than the state of Alaska's original investment of US$18.6 million, and while this may seem a relatively poor rate of return on capital, it must be kept in mind that municipal bond banks are not run as for-profit operations, rather the bond bank's primary purpose is to pursue lower cost loans for the state's municipalities. The Alaska Bond Bank secured over half a billion dollars of funding for Alaskan communities and in the year 2001 alone, the bond bank issued US$50 million in debt and saved the communities an estimated US$4 million in reduced interest costs. The turning of a small profit, while reducing the cost of debt, only emphasises the magnitude of the efficiency gains that these organisations produce.

With the exception of the Municipal Finance Authority of British Columbia, bond banks in Canada are called municipal finance corporations. For the purposes of this paper, municipal finance corporations and the municipal bond banks of the United States will generically be referred to as municipal bond banks, though some differences exist between the Canadian and US institutions. A few of the significant differences are as follows. With the exception of the Municipal Finance Authority of British Columbia, senior Canadian government directly guarantees municipal finance corporation loans. Whereas in the US, senior 160 governmental guarantees are only available on debt issued through the Maine Municipal Bond Bank and the Vermont Municipal Bond Bank. In Canada, with the exception of a few large cities, municipalities located in municipal finance corporation jurisdictions are required to use this facility, whereas in the United States, it is entirely at the discretion of the municipality whether or not to issue debt through the regional bond bank. Some municipal finance corporations have issued debt in foreign currencies; whereas US bond banks have only issued debt in US dollars.

Because of the structure of the municipal finance corporations, in particular the senior governmental guarantee of debt and the requirement for municipality participation, this paper focuses on the US municipal bond bank model. It is believed that the Canadian practices obscure one of the more interesting accomplishments of bond banks: synergistic credit enhancement. If a municipal bond bank operates as an extension of the senior government, then its debt issues are senior governmental debt issues and a municipal bond bank debt issuance should directly result in an increase in the province's overall debt load and should marginally increase the province's cost of capital and could be viewed as an inter-governmental transfer rather than an improvement in efficiency. This model seems inappropriate for an Asian bond bank that lends its credit rating to sovereign governments. Rather than the unrealistic assumption that sovereign Asian governments would willingly assume the debt of other Asian nations, and the moral hazard problems associated with this, we believe the more interesting and important insights gained from the study of municipal bond banks are in the examination of their stand-alone efficiency enhancements, thought to be more distinguishable in the US municipal bond bank model.

Municipal bond banks are structured in a variety of different ways. Because individual bond banks are designed to exploit the cost-saving inefficiencies present in their particular region, bond banks try to organise themselves to focus on their region's greatest inefficiency. Typically, this means focusing the bank's operations to take advantage of either the potential for credit rating arbitrage or the size of the debt issue aspect. Therefore, two broad generalisations can be used to describe bond bank structures.

In one structure, the municipal bond bank issues revenue bonds[1] in the national bondmarket using its own name, and purchases the general 161 obligation bonds of the municipality.[2] When operated in this way, municipal bond banks pass the debt service costs through to the municipalities and the term structure of interest rates for the municipalities is equal to that of the municipal bond banks (Cole and Millar 1982). This allows the municipality to take advantage of the credit rating arbitrage process. In the second operating structure, the municipal bond bank ascertains the borrowing needs of the municipal applicants together and issues debt in one large pool, taking advantage of the increased size of the issue (Figures 7.1 and 7.2).

Figure 7.1 **Bond bank focused on the credit rating effect**

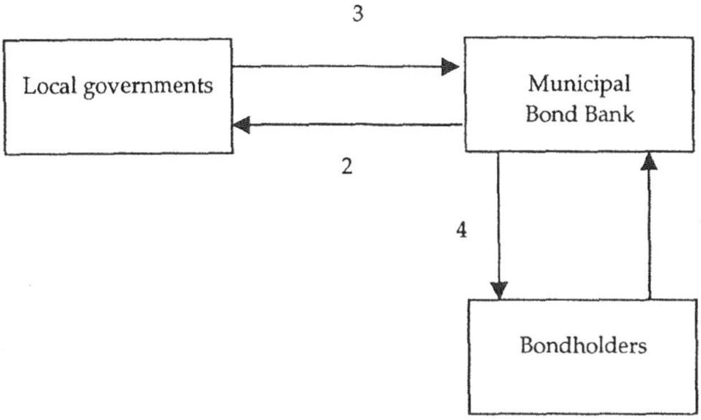

Note: 1. Initial bond offering by municipal bond bank based on municipal bond bank credit rating.
2. Proceeds from municipal bond bank are used to purchase bonds from municipalities.
3. Municipalities pay debt service back to municipal bond bank.
4. Municipal bond bank pays interest and principal to investors from funds repaid by municipalities.
Source: Shinn, P., 1988. 'Bond banks and revolving loan funds', *Government Finance Review,* June:36–37.

How US municipal bond banks operate

In the United States, to be eligible for bond bank participation, municipalities must first fulfil their required jurisdictional obligations for issuing debt. This usually requires obtaining either the approval of the citizens or approval from the bond counsel. The municipality then submits an application to the municipal bond bank.

When making a decision as to whether to include a certain municipality's debt,[3] municipal bond banks examine the same information as the credit ratings agencies. Issues such as the amount of the bond, if the issue was publicly voted on, what assets or taxes (in addition to property taxes) are being pledged, the project feasibility study, the intended sources and uses for the bond bank's funds, the municipality's current outstanding debt, any previous defaults by the municipality, the local economy, the largest employers, the population figures, property tax statistics and the current year's budget all effect the bond bank's decision. Once the bond bank decides to accept the municipality into the debt pool, the municipality pays the same

Figure 7.2 **A bond bank focused on the size of debt issue**

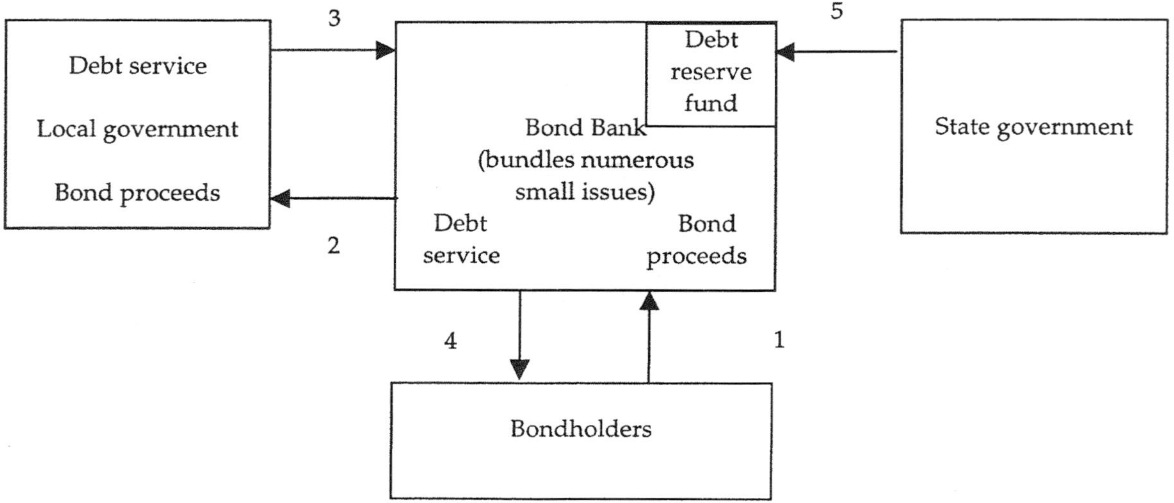

Notes: 1. Initial bond proceeds
2. Bond bank purchases bonds from municipalities
3. Municipalities repay loan to state
4. Bond bank pays debt service to investors from bonds received from municipalities
5. State general or moral obligation to repay reserve fund if bond bank cannot make payments.
Source: Shinn, P., 1988. 'Bond banks and revolving loan funds', *Government Finance Review*, June:36–37.

rate of interest on the borrowed funds as all the other municipalities involved in that debt issuance. That is, after being accepted, the municipality's credit rating ceases to be a distinguishing factor. For an Asian bond bank, adjustments could be made depending upon sovereign credit rating, an Asian credit-rating agency or using a system of tranches of bonds with different cash flow priorities (Rhee 2003).

When the municipal bond bank has accumulated a sufficient amount of debt or the regularly scheduled debt issuance date arrives, the bank floats the issue and in some cases, an additional 10 per cent designated for a reserve or sinking fund. This reserve fund helps lower the cost of debt by reducing the default risk faced by investors. The reserve fund is typically 162 equal to one year's worth of principal and interest payments and can be used in the event of slow pay or default by a municipality (Cole and Millar 1982). The reserve fund is invested in Treasury Securities (Katzman 1980) and 'the interest rate spread between the return on taxable government securities and the tax-exempt bond bank issues is an arbitrage profit for the bond bank' (Kidwell and Rogowski 1983:110).

In order of priority, the collateral behind the municipal bond bank's debt issues are the reserve fund, the full faith and credit of the municipality, a possible lien on state grants in aid to municipality or an 'intercept mechanism', and finally the moral obligation of the state to replenish the reserve fund in case of depletion. Because states typically offer only their moral obligation, municipal bond banks have generally received a credit rating one-notch below senior governmental authority (Katzman 1980).

Because the municipal bond bank is raising funds for the municipality to use in a municipal project, municipal bond bank issues are often free from federal and in many cases state and local taxes. This helps reduce the municipality's debt servicing costs but still attracts investors with equivalent after tax returns.

While requiring the municipality to pay back the principal and interest over the useful life of the asset, some municipal bond banks offer flexibility in their amortisation schedules. The Maine Municipal Bond Bank allows a municipality to 'structure the principal repayments however they would like as long as it coincides with the useful life of the asset being financed' (personal communication with Gregory D. Connors, Maine Municipal Bond Bank). The debt issued by the Municipal Finance Authority of British Columbia is in the form of 'bullets', debt that cannot be called and is due only at maturity.[4] The Municipal Finance Authority of British Columbia and the Bond Bank of Vermont use a level debt service (equal principal and interest payments each year) (Appendix Table 7.1).

The Municipal Finance Authority of British Columbia also offers increased flexibility to its municipalities by allowing them to participate in interest rate swaps, in particular, forward-starting swaps. This flexibility gives the municipality the ability to lock in an affordable rate of interest before the Municipal Finance Authority of British Columbia makes its biannual debt issuance, thereby hedging against a potential rise in interest rates. In addition, access to the swaps market allows the municipality to lock in a fixed rate of interest for a longer or shorter term than the standard Municipal Finance Authority of British Columbia 10-year bond issue.[5]

An additional flexibility offered by municipal bond banks is the use of bond insurance. Municipal bond insurance which has been available since 1971[6] and is a contractual guarantee by a company to pay the bondholder any principal and or interest due at maturity (Gilbert and Pike 1995). Obtaining such insurance usually requires that the municipality have investment grade bonds. Major insurers of bonds include The Ambac Financial Group, The Municipal Bond Insurance Association, Financial Guaranty Insurance Company and Financial Security Assurance Inc.[7]

Financial Security Assurance, the fourth-largest municipal bond insurer, charges premiums based on a number of factors including the type of obligation, the term and average life, rating quality, capital charge for that type of security, market spreads at the time, size of the transaction and Financial Security Assurance's available credit capacity. Premiums are charged as a percentage of total debt service on the bonds and the premium is payable in full, at the time the policy is issued. Premiums range from approximately 10 basis points for Aa/AA rated bonds to 200 basis points for highly structured Baa/BBB bonds (Personal email with Suzanne M. Finnegan, Financial Security Assurance Inc.).

In theory, municipal bond banks should choose to insure debt if the discounted savings from the reduced cost of debt is greater than the cost of the insurance. Such savings are highly dependent upon the credit rating spread between the municipal bond bank and the municipality at the time the debt is issued.

Who benefits the most from participation?

Because of the heterogeneous nature of various municipalities, municipal bond banks offer different benefits to their participants and some municipalities benefit more than do others from bond bank participation. The relative credit rating spread between the state and the stand-alone municipality, plays an important role in whether an municipal bond bank can help a municipality reduce its borrowing cost. Studies indicate that smaller communities with poorer credit ratings benefit the most when issuing debt through municipal bond banks (Cole and Millar 1982, Katzman 1980, Kidwell and Rogowski 1983).

Some large communities, seeing little benefit from joining a municipal bond bank, choose to issue their own debt. A municipality might choose not to use the services of a municipal bond bank when they have concerns about implicitly reducing their own debt capacity, improving liquidity and name recognition for debt issued in their own name, as well as a desire to develop their own credit history. This may be a problem for an Asian bond bank. Better rated countries such as Singapore, Hong Kong SAR and Chinese Taipei may not see the benefit of joining such an organisation, seeing little benefit for themselves.

The two methods available for selling debt to an underwriter, or making an initial public offering, are the negotiated process and the competitive bid process. Empirical studies have found that the competitive bid process typically yields a lower cost of debt than does the negotiated process. However, municipalities with a poor credit rating and municipalities that only need to issue a small amount of debt may have no alternative but to issue debt in a negotiated process. Additionally, because of the composition and complexity of bond bank issues, and the presence of only a few underwriters who engage in bond bank sales, most bond banks sell their debt issues to underwriters in a negotiated process as well. This group includes the Maine and Vermont Municipal Bond Banks (Kidwell and Rogowski 1983).[8]

However, because a large municipality can choose how it will sell its bonds to the underwriter, a direct comparison between municipal issues and bond bank issues may not be appropriate. A municipality with a credit rating equal to the bond bank may have greater savings if it chooses to issue debt on its own in a competitively bid auction.

Kidwell and Rogowski's 1983 study of the Vermont and Maine Municipal Bond Banks showed that the only municipalities that did not benefit from municipal bond bank participation were those involved in competitively bid auctions with credit ratings of Aaa and issues over US$5 million, and municipalities with Aa ratings and debt issues over US$40 million. Savings for smaller and more poorly rated municipalities ranged up to 154 basis points. That is, it was only the large, competitively bid, bond issues from issuers with Aa ratings or better that did not benefit from bond bank participation.

With such large reductions in the cost of debt, one must ask whether there are hidden costs associated with municipal bond banks or can one attribute the entire reduction in the cost of debt to improvements in efficiency? Examination of this issue has focused on whether perceived increases in the debt load of the state might increase the overall cost of capital for the region. In the United States, municipal bond banks are separate legal entities and in most cases, the senior government is not financially liable for the bank's actions.

However, such a situation may exist if the bondmarket participants mistakenly assume that the municipal bond bank's debt is an implicit obligation of the state. In theory, this could adversely affect the cost of borrowing for the state and indirectly penalise municipalities who are not using the municipal bond bank. This could occur if investors required an increased premium in compensation for the perceived increase in the state's debt load. Empirical evidence is far from definitive in this matter.

In the United States, municipal bond banks are legal entities separate from the state in which they operate. Typically, the full faith and credit of the bank is pledged to the payments of principal, redemption premium and interest, but this is not a 'legally enforceable obligation upon the State' (Maine Municipal Bond Bank 2000:3) though the state often pledges its moral obligation to the maintenance of a debt service reserve for all of the bond bank's bonds(Alaska Bond Bank 1999).[9]

While municipalities rarely default, problems have arisen. In particular is the case of Leukerbad, Switzerland in 1998. Leukerbad, a small ski and tourist town, unwisely borrowed to the point where it could no longer make its interest payments and defaulted. The Swiss government, under no legal obligation to help, stayed away from the situation. Several factors make this less likely to happen when a bond bank is involved. First, bond banks examine the ability of the municipality to repay its borrowings. If the bond bank believes the community cannot repay its debt, the bond bank will refuse to issue bonds and the community will need seek alternative methods of raising capital or forgo their intended project. Secondly, the bond bank is a separate entity from the state of government. Should a community fail to repay its debt, and the bond bank also default, the chain of liability stops with the bond bank and the state need not step in and make the interest and principal repayments for the bondholders, thereby limiting the liability of the state.

Cooperative borrowing in Europe

Although European countries typically have special banks or agencies that lend to municipalities, cooperative borrowing agencies also exist. Two major cooperative borrowers in Europe are Kommunivest, in Sweden, and Bank Nederlandse Gemeenten in the Netherlands.

Kommunivest began its cooperative program in 1986. Currently there are 111 Swedish municipalities and three county councils that are members. Like their Canadian counterparts, Kommunivest diversifies its operations to include borrowings from foreign capital markets and in foreign currencies;[10] however, such borrowings do not enjoy the tax-free status received by US issues. Kommunivest borrowings are divided among Swedish, other European and Japanese capital markets. The bank does all the documentation, swaps and hedging required for the debt. Moody's current credit rating for Kommunivest is Aa1, the same as that for the Kingdom of Sweden.

Issues of assimilation between better credit rated municipalities and more poorly rated municipalities have arisen in Sweden. The two largest cities in Sweden, Stockholm and Gothenburg, have Aa1 ratings (the same as Kommunivest) and both have refused to join the cooperative, believing that economically stronger regions have little, or nothing to gain by joining. Rather these larger, better credit rated communities believe they are subsidising the borrowing of weaker municipalities. The issue of wanting to establish their own credit history and the desire to develop liquidity and name recognition for their own debt may further deter municipalities from joining the cooperative. Problems have arisen in Germany as well. Though written into the German constitution that various *länder*, or regions, shall be mutually supportive, economically stronger regions are fighting to avoid lending their stronger credit ratings to the economically weaker regions, in particular the newer regions in eastern Germany. These examples demonstrate the difficulties in enticing bigger, and better-rated, regions to join in cooperative borrowing arrangements.

Potential applications to Asia

International credit rating agencies have given many Asian governments relatively low credit ratings. One of the basic ideas of diversification is that whenever the returns of individual securities are not perfectly correlated, the risk of a portfolio of those same securities can be reduced. This same idea can be applied to the pooling and reselling of bonds from multiple countries. Because the economies of Asian economies are quite different, the risk of the overall portfolio of bonds from Asian countries should have a better risk–return tradeoff and therefore a lower cost of capital for the bond banks bonds. This saving could be passed on to the borrowing countries.

While Asian sovereign issuers are larger than small US municipalities, small corporate issuers could eventually be allowed to issue bonds through the bond bank. Such involvement with the bond bank's bonds could significantly increase the secondary market liquidity of the corporation's debt and reduce borrowing costs.

Finally, bond banks have another practical advantage; that is, the extent to which the borrower is liable for the debt of other borrowers. It seems unlikely that any country would be freely willing guarantee the debt of another. Bond bank bonds are the bond bank's responsibility to repay, not the government of the borrowing country, although it is possible that the country might lose its initial investment in the bond bank.

Conclusion

Municipal bond banks first appeared in Canada in 1956 and in the United States in 1970. Since that time, municipal bond banks have been offering a unique and advantageous way for communities to finance municipal projects. Municipal bond banks operate as credit enhancing organisations that pool multiple municipalities' borrowing needs into a single issue.

Municipal bond banks are efficiency enhancing organisations, which are often able to significantly reduce the cost of debt for small, unrated or poorly rated municipalities. The savings of the municipality are highly dependent upon its borrowing needs and the relative credit rating spread between the state and municipality at the time the debt is issued.

Bond banks are heterogeneous in structure and operation, offering varying degrees of flexibility in their amortisation schedules and the use of swaps. Municipal bond banks are able to improve the borrowing costs for the municipalities primarily through credit rating arbitrage, that is, lending funds obtained using their better credit rating to more poorly rated municipalities, although municipal bond banks also lower the cost of debt through the economies of scale in the underwriting process and knowledge of capital markets.

Many Asian countries have poorly rated government debt and this increases their cost of debt. A credit enhancing program modelled along the lines of a bond bank could help Asian countries and firms reduce their cost of capital. Because pooled Asian bonds are essentially a portfolio of bonds, and the price movements of various Asian economy bonds are less than perfectly correlated, bond bank bonds could produce a lower risk portfolio and result in a lower cost of capital for the bond bank which could be passed along to the borrowing countries.

Notes

1 Municipal bond bank's bonds are revenue bonds because of the source of their principal and interest payments are the cash flows generated by the municipalities.

2 Investigation into the proceeds generated by revenue bonds versus the proceeds generated by general obligation bonds (general obligation bonds tend to enjoy a lower interest rate than comparable revenue bonds) have found that the savings from bond bank participation have surpassed the losses of issuing revenue bonds instead of general obligation bonds. Additionally, a municipal bond bank will often incorporate a municipality's revenue bonds in its debt offering.

3 In the United States, municipal bond banks typically have the authority to exclude a municipality if it is felt such a municipality would significantly detract from the marketability of its bonds. An example where a municipal bond bank might not want to include a certain municipality's debt is if the municipality's borrowing needs were very large, swamping the municipal bond bank's credit capacity and thereby damaging its ability to serve other municipalities.

4 If the Municipal Finance Authority of British Columbia issued callable debt, investors would require, at a minimum an equal, but more commonly, a higher rate of return. This difference between callable and non-callable debt is referred to as the 'option adjusted spread'.

5 An 'extension swap' is a special type of forward swap. It allows the municipality to lock in a fixed rate of interest beyond the original tenor of the swap.

6 The first use of municipal bond insurance was in 1971. The Greater Juneau (Alaska) Borough Medical Arts Building General Obligation Bonds were insured for a par value of $650,000.

7 In 1986, Financial Security Assurance Inc. was the first bond insurer to guarantee an international security.

8 In recent years, more than 80 per cent of the dollar volume of municipal initial public offerings has been sold through negotiated bond sales (Chang 2000).

9 The Alaska Bond Bank's Annual Report notes that, although it pledges its moral support, the state 'is not obligated to pay principal or interest thereon. Nor does the State pledge its taxing power to the bonds' (Alaska Bond Bank 1999).

10 It is believed that the future currency payments are swapped back to home currency to reduce the exchange rate risk.

Appendix Table 7.1 **Example of a payment structure of the Municipal Finance Authority of British Columbia**

20 year term, 5 %Capitalisation rate, Principal: 1,000,000.00, Interest rate: 5 per cent, S/F factor: 0.030242587

	Principal payment	Interest payment	Total payment	Acturial	Reducing balance
Yr 1 Semi-annual		25,000.00	25,000.00		1,000,000.00
Yr 1 Annual	30,242.59	25,000.00	55,242.59		969,757.41
Yr 2 Semi-annual		25,000.00	25,000.00		969,757.41
Yr 2 Annual	30,242.59	25,000.00	55,242.59	1,512.13	938,002.70
Yr 3 Semi-annual		25,000.00	25,000.00		938,002.70
Yr 3 Annual	30,242.59	25,000.00	55,242.59	3,099.87	904,660.24
Yr 4 Semi-annual		25,000.00	25,000.00		904,660.24
Yr 4 Annual	30,242.59	25,000.00	55,242.59	4,766.99	869,650.67
Yr 5 Semi-annual		25,000.00	25,000.00		869,650.67
Yr 5 Annual	30,242.59	25,000.00	55,242.59	6,517.47	832,890.62
Yr 6 Semi-annual		25,000.00	25,000.00		832,890.62
Yr 6 Annual	30,242.59	25,000.00	55,242.59	8.355.47	794,292.56
Yr 7 Semi-annual		25,000.00	25,000.00		794,292.56
Yr 7 Annual	30,242.59	25,000.00	55,242.59	10,285.37	753,764.60
Yr 8 Semi-annual		25,000.00	25,000.00		753,764.60
Yr 8 Annual	30,242.59	25,000.00	55,242.59	12,311.77	711,210.24
Yr 9 Semi-annual		25,000.00	25,000.00		711,210.24
Yr 9 Annual	30,242.59	25,000.00	55,242.59	14,439.49	666,528.17
Yr 10 Semi-annual		25,000.00	25,000.00		666,528.17
Yr 10 Annual	30,242.59	25,000.00	55,242.59	16,673.59	619,611.99
Yr 11 Semi-annual		25,000.00	25,000.00		619,611.99
Yr 11 Annual	30,242.59	25,000.00	55,242.59	19,019.40	570,350.00

Yr 12 Semi-annual		25,000.00	25,000.00		570,350.00
Yr 12 Annual	30,242.59	25,000.00	55,242.59	21,482.50	518,624.91
Yr 13 Semi-annual		25,000.00	25,000.00		518,624.91
Yr 13 Annual	30,242.59	25,000.00	55,242.59	24,068.75	464,313.57
Yr 14 Semi-annual		25,000.00	25,000.00		464,313.57
Yr 14 Annual	30,242.59	25,000.00	55,242.59	26,784.32	407,286.66
Yr 15 Semi-annual		25,000.00	25,000.00		407,286.66
Yr 15 Annual	30,242.59	25,000.00	55,242.59	29,635.67	347,408.41
Yr 16 Semi-annual		25,000.00	25,000.00		347,408.41
Yr 16 Annual.	30,242.59	25,000.00	55,242.59	32,629.58	284.536.24
Yr 17 Semi-annual		25,000.00	25,000.00		284.536.24
Yr 17 Annual	30,242.59	25,000.00	55,242.59	35,773.19	218,520.47
Yr 18 Semi-annual		25,000.00	25,000.00		218,520.47
Yr 18 Annual	30,242.59	25,000.00	55,242.59	39,073.98	149,203.90
Yr 19 Semi-annual		25,000.00	25,000.00		149,203.90
Yr 19 Annual	30,242.59	25,000.00	55,242.59	42,539.80	76,421.51
Yr 20 Semi-annual		25,000.00	25,000.00		76,421.51
Yr 20 Annual	30,242.59	25,000.00	55,242.59	46,178.92	(0.00)
Total	604,851.74	1,000,000.00	1,604,851.74	395,148.26	

References

Aghion, P., Bacchetta, P. and Banerjee, A., 2001. *A corporate balance-sheet approach to currency crises*, CEPR Discussion Paper 3092, Center for Economic Policy Research, Washington, DC.

Ahn, S. and Chan-Lee, J., 2001. *Informational quality of financial systems and economic development: an indicators approach for East Asia*, ADB Institute Research Paper No. 20, Asian Development Bank Institute, Tokyo.

Alaska Bond Bank, 1999. *Annual Report 1999*, Alaska Bond Bank, Juneau, AK.

——, 2001. *Annual Report 2001*, Alaska Bond Bank, Juneau, AK.

Aoki, M., 2000. *A note on the role of banking in developing economies in the aftermath of the East Asian crisis*, Discussion paper for Roundtable discussion on Capital and Labor Markets, World Bank, Paris.

Asian Bankers Association, 2003. Promoting the development of securitization and credit guarantee, Position Paper of Asian Bankers Association, 21 March, Manila.

Asian Development Bank, 1999. *Compendium of Sound Practices Guidelines to Facilitate the Development of Domestic Bond Markets in APEC Member Countries*, Asian Development Bank, Manila.

Bae, K. and Park, Y., 2002. Financial liberalization and economic integration in East Asia, Paper presented at the PECC Finance Forum, Honolulu, 11–13 August.

Bank for International Settlements, 2002. *Insolvency arrangements and contract enforceability*, Report of the Contact Group on the Legal and Institutional Underpinnings of the International Financial System, International Monetary Fund, Washington, DC. Available online at http://www.imf.org/external/np/g10/2002/pdf/120502.pdf.

Barnhill, T.M., Maxwell, W.F. and Shenkman, M.R., 1998. *High-Yield Bonds: market structure, portfolio management and credit risk modeling*, McGraw-Hill, New York.

Bergsten, Fred C. and Yung Chul Park, 2002. *Toward creating a regional monetary arrangement in East Asia*, ADB Institute Research Paper No. 50, Tokyo. Available online from http://www.adbi.org/PDF/wp/rp50.pdf.

Borden, S. and Sarkar, A., 1996. 'Securitizing property catastrophe risk', *Current Issues in Economics and Finance*, 2(9). Available at http://http://www.newyorkfed.org/research/current_issues/ci2-9.pdf.

Canter, M.S., Cole, J.B. and Sandor, R.L., 1997. 'Insurance derivatives: a new asset class for the capital markets and a new hedging tool for the insurance industry', *Journal of Applied Corporate Finance*, 10(3):68–83.

Chaipravat, O., 2003. Asian bond status report, Presentation at the ASEAN+3 High-Level Seminar on Fostering Bond Markets in Asia, Tokyo, 1 March.

——, Supapol, B.B. and Sangsubhan, K., 2003. Regional self-help and support mechanisms: beyond the CMI, Paper submitted to the ASEAN Secretariat, Jakarta.

Chang, R., 2000. Overview of US municipal bondmarkets, Paper presented at the Conference on Development of an Indonesian Municipal Bond Market, Jakarta.

Cole, C.W. and Millar, J.A., 1982. 'The impact of municipal bond banking on municipal interest costs', *Financial Management*, II(1):70–76.

Crockett, A.D., 2002. Capital flows in East Asia since the crisis, Paper presented at the ASEAN+3 High Level Seminar on Management of Short-term Capital Flow and Capital Account Liberalization, Beijing.

Dalla, I., 2002. Asset-backed securities markets in selected East Asian countries, World Bank, Washington, DC (unpublished).

Department of the Treasury/Federal Reserve Board, 2004. Major foreign holders of treasury securities, United States Department of the Treasury, Washington, DC. Available online from http://www.ustreas.gov/tic/mfh.txt.

Demirguc-Kunt, A. and Levine, R. (eds), 2001. *Financial structure and economic growth: a cross-country comparison of banks, markets and development*, MIT Press, Cambridge and London.

Duisenberg, W.F., 1999. The role of capital markets and financing in the Euro Area, Speech delivered at the Waarborgfonds Sociale Woningbouw, Utrecht, 14 June.

Eichengreen, B., and Hausmann, R., 1999a. *Exchange rates and financial fragility*, NBER Working Paper No. 7418, National Bureau of Economic Research, Cambridge, MA.

——, 1999b. 'Exchange rates and financial fragility', *New Challenges for Monetary Policy*, Federal Reserve Bank of Kansas City, Kansas City: 329–68.

Eichengreen, B., 2002. Whither monetary and financial cooperation in Asia?, Paper presented at the 2002 APFA/PACAP/FMA Finance Conference (unpublished).

——, Hausmann, R. and Panizza, U., 2002. Original sin: the pain, the mystery, and the road to redemption, Paper presented at the conference Currency and Maturity Matchmaking: Redeeming Debt from Original Sin, Inter-American Development Bank, Washington, DC, November.

—— and Park, Yung-chul, 2003. Why has there been less financial integration in Asia than in Europe?, Paper presented at the Second Annual Conference of the PECC Finance Forum, Hua Hin.

Ferri, G. and Liu, Li-Gang, 2002. 'Do global credit rating agencies think globally? The information content of firm ratings around the world', *Royal Economic Society Annual Conference 2002*, Royal Economic Society, London.

Fitch IBCA, 2003a. *Latin American Structured Finance 2002 Year in Review and Outlook*, Fitch Ratings, New York. Available online at http://www.fitchibca.com/corporate/reports/report.cfm?rpt_id=167924.

——, 2003b. *US Financial Guarantors and Reinsurers*, Fitch Ratings, New York.

Fukuchi, A., 2003. 'Trend of Asian bond market', *Tokyo-Mitsubishi Review*, October:1–8.

Gilbert, M. and Pike, R., 1995. 'Credit enhancement of municipal debt', *Canadian Public Administration*, 38(2):195–203.

Giovannini Group, 2001. *Cross-border Clearing and Settlement Arrangements in the European Union*, European Union, Brussels.

——, 2003. *Second Report on EU Clearing and Settlement Arrangements*, European Union, Brussels.

Goodman, L.S. and Fabozzi, F.J., 2002. *Collateralized Debt Obligations: structures and analysis*, John Wiley & Sons, Hoboken, NJ.

Greenspan, A., 1999. Lessons from the global crises, remarks before the World Bank Group and the International Monetary Fund, Annual Meetings Program of Seminars, Washington, DC, 17 September. Available online at http://www.federalreserve.gov/Boarddocs/Speeches/1999/199909272.htm.

Haggard, S., 2000. *The Political Economy of the Asian Financial Crisis*, Institute for International Economics, Washington, DC.

Hohensee, M., 2001. 'The Malaysian bond market', *Global Markets Research*, Deutsche Bank, Frankfurt.

Hong Kong Monetary Authority (HKMA), 2000a. US dollar clearing system goes live, Press release, Hong Kong Monetary Authority, Hong Kong, 17 August. Available online at http://www.info.gov.hk/hkma/eng/press/2000/20000817e4_index.htm.

——, 2000b. US dollar clearing system: full implementation from 18 December 2000, Press release, Hong Kong Monetary Authority, Hong Kong, 14 December.

——, 2001. 'Cost–benefit analysis of developing debt markets', *Quarterly Bulletin*, November:1–18.

——, 2002. Further study on securitization and credit enhancement in Asia, Hong Kong Monetary Authority, Hong Kong (unpublished).

Ikeya, M., 2001. *Securitization market in Asia (excluding Japan) stalls: public commitment and initiatives to be tested*, R&I Asian Focus Special Report,

Ratings and Investment Information Inc., Tokyo. Available online at http://www.r-i.co.jp/eng/release/nr_international/asia010904.pdf.

International Monetary Fund, 2002. *Global Financial Stability Report: market developments and issues*, International Monetary Fund, Washington, DC. Available online at http://www.imf.org/External/Pubs/FT/GFSR/2002/03/index.htm.

——, 2003. *Global Financial Stability Report: market developments and issues*, International Monetary Fund, Washington, DC. Available online at http://www.imf.org/External/Pubs/FT/GFSR/2003/01/index.htm.

—— and World Bank, 2001. *Developing Government Bond Markets: a handbook*, World Bank and International Monetary Fund, Washington, DC.

Independent Evaluation Office of the International Monetary Fund, 2003. *IMF and Recent Capital Account Crises: Indonesia, Korea, Brazil*, Evaluation Report, September, International Monetary Fund, Washington, DC.

—— (various issues). *International Financial Statistics*, International Monetary Fund, Washington, DC.

Ito, T., 2003a. *New ideas needed to foster Asian bond markets*, Glocom Platform, Japanese Institute of Global Communications, Toyko. Available online at http://www.glocom.org/opinions/essays/20030717_ito_new/index.html.

——, 2003b. Asian basket currency (ABC) bonds, Paper presented at the ASEAN+3 High-Level Seminar on Fostering Bond Markets in Asia, Tokyo, 1 March.

——, 2003c. Promoting Asian basket currency (ABC) bonds, presented at the Voluntary Working Group Meeting of the Asian Bond Markets Initiative, Tokyo, 17 June.

Jang, W., Kim, C., Lee, S. and Park, H., 2002. 'The creation of the ACU and its application to the bond market', in C. Han Gwang and W. Yunjong (eds), *Currency Union in East Asia*, Korea Institute for International Economic Policy, Seoul.

Katzman, M.T., 1980. 'Municipal bond banking: the diffusion of a public-finance innovation', *National Tax Journal*, 33:149–60.

Kidwell, D.S. and Rogowski, R.J., 1983. 'Bond banks: a state assistance program that helps reduce new issue borrowing costs', *Public Administration Review*, 43(2):108–13.

Kolb, R.W., 1997. *Futures, Options and Swaps*, Blackwell Publishers, Malden, Massachusetts.

Krueger, A.O., 2001. A new approach to sovereign debt restructuring, Speech presented at Indian Council for Research on International Economic Relations, Delhi, 20 December. Available online at http://www.imf.org/external/pubs/ft/exrp/sdrm/eng/sdrm.pdf.

——, 2002. Sovereign debt restructuring mechanism—one year later, Speech presented at the European Commission, Brussels, 10 December. Available online at http://www.imf.org/external/np/speeches/2002/121002.htm.

Krugman, P., 1998. What happened to Asia?, Massachusetts Institute of Technology, Boston (unpublished).

La Porta, R. Lopez-de-Silanes, F., Shleifer, A., Vishny, R., 1998. 'Law and finance', *Journal of Political Economy*, 106:1113–55.

Latza, 1997. 'Risk securitization growth expected', *National Underwriter*, 14 July.

Levine, R., 2000. Bank-based or market-based financial systems: which is better?, Paper presented at the conference on Financial Structure and Economic Development, World Bank, Washington, DC, 1 August.

Levine, R., Loayza, and Beck, T., 2000. 'Financial Intermediation and Growth: Causality and Causes', *Journal of Monetary Economics*, 46(1):31–77.

Lim Hng K., 2003. East Asian capital markets: challenging times, Keynote address delivered at the Euromoney 10th Asia Pacific Issuers and Investors Forum, Singapore, 18 March.

Maine Municipal Bond Bank, 2000. *Series A and B bonds prospectus*, Maine Municipal Bond Bank, Maine.

McCauley, R.N., Fung, S. and Gadanecz, B., 2002. 'Integrating the finances of East Asia', *BIS Quarterly Review*, December:83–95.

Monetary Authority of Singapore, 2001a. *Annual Report*, Monetary Authority of Singapore, Singapore.

——, 2001b. *Survey of the Singapore Corporate Debt Market*, Monetary Authority of Singapore, Singapore.

——, 2003. *Survey of the Singapore Corporate Debt Market*, Monetary Authority of Singapore, Singapore. Available online at http://www.mas.gov.sg/singfinsec/download/2002DebtSurvey.pdf.

Moody's Investors Service, 2002. 'Malaysia's debt capital markets assume new importance', Special Comments, *Global Credit Research*, New York.

Ng, E., 2000. 'Central Provident Fund in Singapore: a capital market boost or a drag?' in *Rising to the Challenge in Asia: a study of financial markets: volume 3—sound practices*, Asian Development Bank, Manila:55–80. Available online at http://www.adb.org/Documents/Books/Rising_to_the_Challenge/Sound_Practices/sing-cpf.pdf.

Ngiam, K. and Loh, L., 2002. *Developing a viable corporate bond market: the Singapore experience*, Institute of Southeast Asian Studies, Singapore.

Oh, G. and Park, J., 2003. Fostering Asian bond markets using securitization and credit guarantee, Paper presented at the Voluntary Working Group Meeting of the Asian Bond Markets Initiative, Tokyo, 16 June.

——, Park, D., and Yang, D., 2003. *How to mobilize the Asian savings within the region: securitization and credit enhancement for the development of East Asia's bond market*, Working Paper No. 03-02, South Korea Institute for International Economic Policy, Seoul.

Park, Yung Chul, 2002. *Prospects for financial integration in exchange rate policy coordination in East Asia*, Research Paper No. 48, Asian Development Bank Institute, Tokyo.

Park, Y., 2003. How to develop regional bond markets in East Asia, Proposal to the Second Annual Conference of the PECC Finance Forum, Issues and Challenges for Regional Financial Cooperationin the Asia Pacific, Hua Hin.

Quaden, G., 1999. The impact of the single currency on the financial markets and the international role of the euro, Speech delivered at Belgian Banker's Association meeting, Brussels, 14 October.

Rhee, S.G., 2000. 'Rising to Asia's challenge: enhanced role of capital markets', in *Rising to the Challenge in Asia: a study of financial markets: volume 1—an overview*, Asian Development Bank, Manila:107–74. Available online at http://www.adb.org/Documents/Books/Rising_to_the_Challenge/Overview/3-over-cap.pdf.

——, 2001. 'Further reforms after the "Big Bang": the Japanese Government bond market', in *Bond Market Development in Asia*, Organization for Economic Co-operation and Development, Paris:217–36.

——, 2003. The structure and characteristics of East Asian bond markets, Paper presented at the Second Annual Conference of the PECC Finance Forum, Issues and Challenges for Regional Financial Cooperationin the Asia Pacific, Hua Hin, July. Available online at http://www.pecc.org/finance/forum2003/Session3-Rhee(rev-20-07-03).pdf.

—— and Stone, G., 2003. *Credit enhancement for regional bond markets: an application of cooperative borrowing under municipal bond banks*, Working Paper, University of Hawaii, Honolulu.

Shin, M., 2003. Development of securitization and credit guarantee markets for bond market development, Keynote address at the APEC High-Level Policy Dialogue, Seoul, 3 April. Available online at http://www.adb.org/Media/Articles/2003/1930_Keynote_Address_Mr_Myoung_Ho_Shin/.

Shinn, P., 1988. 'Bond banks and revolving loan funds', *Government Finance Review*, June:36–37.

Subiyantoro, H. and Ginting, L. S., 2003. Indonesian government bonds market development, Paper presented at Asian Bond Symposium, Keio University, Tokyo, February.

Taniguchi, T., 2003. Asian Bond Markets Initiative, Keynote speech delivered at the ASEAN+3 High-Level Seminar on Fostering Bond Markets in Asia, Tokyo, 1 March.

Tsang, D., 1998. Asian Bond Market, Speech at the Asian Debt Conference, Singapore, 6 July. Available online at www.info.gov.hk/hkma/eng/speeches/ speechs/hondonald/speech_060798b.htm - 31k

Watmore, G., 2003. Asset securitization: growth potential in Asia, prepared for the Voluntary Working Group Meeting of the Asian Bond Markets Initiative, Tokyo, 17 June.

Wong, M. and Ho, R., 2003. Road map for building the institutional foundation for regional bond market in East Asia: credit insurers, ABS corporations and Asian bond funds, Paper presented at the Second Annual Conference of the PECC Finance Forum, Issues and Challenges for Regional Financial Cooperationin the Asia Pacific, Hua Hin, July. Available online at http://www.pecc.org/finance/forum2003/Session3-Ho-Wong.pdf.

Yamagami, H., 2003. 'Asian bond market—a scheme for ABS issuers', Japanese Bankers' Association, *Kin-yu*, November:2–15.

Zorn, K.C and Towfighi, S., 1986. 'Not all bond banks are created equal', *Public Budgeting and Finance*, 6(3):57–69.

Index

Made in United States
Orlando, FL
04 November 2026

90206770R00107